Reunion in Barsaloi

Corinne Hofmann

Born in 1960 of a French mother and a German father in Frauenfeld in the Swiss canton of Thurgau, Corinne Hofmann had an international bestseller with *The White Masai*, an autobiographical account of her life in Kenya, which has since been translated into more than twenty languages and has spawned a film adaptation, seen by more than one million people when released in Germany in 2005. Her second book, *Zurück aus Afrika* (*Back from Africa*) described her attempt to start a new life back in Switzerland. An English translation will be published by Bliss Books in 2007. She has lived for several years with her daughter near Lake Lugano.

Corinne Hofmann

Reunion in Barsaloi

Translated from the German by Peter Millar

BLISS BOOKS
LONDON

Arcadia Books Ltd
15-16 Nassau Street
London W1W 7AB

www.arcadiabooks.co.uk

First published in the United Kingdom 2006, by Bliss Books, an imprint of Arcadia Books
This B format edition first published in the United Kingdom 2007
Sixth edition, April 2009
Copyright © A1 Verlag GmbH, München
First published by A1 Verlag, München as Wiedersehen in Barsaloi in 2005
Translation © Peter Millar 2006

A catalogue record for this book is available from the British Library.

ISBN 978-1-905147-40-3

Typeset in Bembo by Basement Press
Printed in Finland by WS Bookwell

Arcadia Books supports English PEN, the fellowship of writers who work together to promote literature and its understanding. English PEN upholds writers' freedoms in Britain and around the world, challenging political and cultural limits on free expression.
To find out more, visit www.englishpen.org or contact
English PEN, 6-8 Amwell Street, London EC1R 1UQ

Arcadia Books distributors are as follows:

in the UK and elsewhere in Europe:
Turnaround Publishers Services
Unit 3, Olympia Trading Estate
Coburg Road London N22 6TZ

in the USA and Canada:
Independent Publishers Group
814 N. Franklin St. Chicago, IL 60610

in Australia:
Tower Books
PO Box 213 Brookvale, NSW 2100

in New Zealand:
Addenda
Box 78224 Grey Lynn Auckland

in South Africa:
Quartet Sales and Marketing
PO Box 1218 Northcliffe Johannesburg 2115

Arcadia Books is the *Sunday Times* Small Publisher of the Year

Acknowledgements

I would like to say thank you to everyone who made my 'journey back in time' possible, in particular: Lketinga, Mama, James and all the other members of my wonderful African family, as well as all the inhabitants of Barsaloi who welcomed me back into their midst so warmly, Father Giuliani who showed us his hospitality and gave us an insight into many of the problems facing Samburu culture today, the staff of Constantin Film, who allowed me a glimpse behind the scenes of the making of 'my' movie, my publisher Albert Völkmann who came along on the trip as a 'fatherly friend' and Klaus Kamphausen who made the arrangements for our trip and took the photographs and video, my readers who have shared my life and that of my African family and who gave me the courage to go back to Barsaloi, and last but by no means least Napirai who, despite early misgivings, understood my reasons and let me make the trip.

Translator's note

Corinne and Lketinga communicated with each other in what she calls their 'special language', essentially a form of broken English, which neither spoke fluently, augmented by sign language and a very few phrases in the Samburu language, Maa. Throughout the book Corinne occasionally includes a few snatches of conversation in this basic rather stilted English. Rather than improve these I have, in this book as in *The White Masai*, left them in the original. When she reverts to normal, idiomatic German, I have however, of course, used normal, idiomatic English.

For my African family

Going Back

It all seems so long ago now. It is almost fourteen years since I fled Kenya with my daughter Napirai, then only eighteen months old, and now I'm sitting in a plane on my way back to Nairobi for the first time. I'm an emotional wreck. One minute my stomach is churning with excitement, the next I'm so nervous my hands have gone damp and clammy. I could collapse in tears one second and burst out laughing the next.

All sorts of questions are rattling around in my head. What will I make of my old home? How much will have changed? Will anything still be the same? Will 'progress' and the hectic pace of life that goes with it have changed Kenya so much that I won't recognize the tiny village of Barsaloi in the north of the country or the people who live there now? Fourteen years ago there was only the Mission building, eight or so wooden huts, our breezeblock shop and a few *manyattas*, the traditional cow dung-plastered homes of the Samburu tribes-people.

Sitting next to me in the plane is Albert Völkmann, my publisher, who's coming with me in the role of a 'fatherly friend', as he puts it, and Klaus Kamphausen, a photographer and film cameraman who has come along to make a visual record of our trip. I'm relieved and glad not to be embarking on an adventure like this alone.

During the flight I keep thinking about all the people I haven't seen for so long: my mother-in-law, for whom to this day I have enormous respect, my ex-husband Lketinga, James, his little brother, Saguna, his niece. I'm also hoping to see Father Giuliani, who on more than one occasion saved my life, as long as we can find his new Mission. I just hope it all goes well and it's not all going to fall apart the minute we land.

Eventually I doze off and when I open my eyes a couple of hours later there are red and orange stripes across the sky, exactly the same sort of dawn that greeted me two years ago at the end of a long, exhausting climb up Mount Kilimanjaro in Tanzania. The difference is that back then, sitting at Stella Point 18,000 feet above sea level, I was absolutely worn out, whereas now I'm no more than a little stiff and uncomfortable in my aircraft seat. Gazing out at the bare mountaintops beneath us in the dawn, I drift slowly off to sleep again.

But then, just about an hour before we land, I have a panic attack that almost makes me sick, and I pray to God it'll all be okay. Through the window now I can see the endless expanse of the Kenyan plains. Here and there I can even make out the occasional circular corral – a few *manyattas* grouped together and surrounded with a thicket fence to protect them from wild animals.

Maybe we're even flying over Barsaloi itself? I think how often I used to sit outside our *manyatta* with Mama, looking up at the sky. Whenever we saw a plane pass over she would ask how these 'iron birds', as she called them, could find their way without any paths or lights up there. Is there a chance she's sitting down there now, looking up at the sky in the knowledge that I'm on my way?

All at once I want to jump out of the plane and parachute down to them. Sitting there lost in my thoughts, I soak in the vista of dried-up river beds wending their way across the dust-red earth and the green fringe of trees that, despite the drought, still marks their banks. A few minutes later the plane begins the slow loop of its descent towards the runway in Nairobi.

The Big Decision

For months before I could set out on this journey I had gone over and over the same argument in my head: am I doing the right thing? So many things keep happening and changing my life that with hindsight it seems as if it had all been preordained.

Over the years I had time and again made approaches by telephone to the Kenyan Embassy in Switzerland and the German Embassy in Nairobi to try and find out what could be done to have my divorce from my Samburu husband, which had gone through in Switzerland, recognized in Kenya. Every time the answer had been the same: I would have to engage a Kenyan lawyer but first and foremost I would have to get my husband's agreement. Lketinga (whom I had left in Mombasa on the coast) was now once again living in northern Kenya and had been married for years to a young woman from his tribe. There could simply be no question of asking him to come to Nairobi, not least because he wouldn't see the point of it. Things were going fine for him; and as men could have more than one wife, divorce was simply unheard of among the Samburu.

But as that meant I would still have to get his permission as my husband before I could leave the country again, I simply left things as they were, reconciled to never being able to visit Kenya again. Nonetheless, my thoughts often returned to my family there, above all my mother-in-law, my daughter's grandmother. With the thought that we could leave it a few years until Napirai was an adult and expressed a wish to visit her father and then we would find a way around things, I simply put my European divorce papers back in the drawer.

For the whole of 2003 I was busy promoting my book, enjoying myself hugely touring as an author and giving readings. Work was also well in progress now on turning the book into a film and that meant I had to travel to Munich often for consultations on the script. It was good that they let me make comments and suggestions and listened to what I had to say; we ended up working closely together, which at least meant I found it easier to live with the occasional changes that were made for dramatic effect.

Nonetheless, it wasn't easy to have to see whole chunks of my own life re-enacted with different names while things that happened to me were often cut out or changed. Some of the scenes left me in tears, aware of how much it all mattered to me, but at the same time proud that an important part of my life was going to be transposed to the cinema screen. I was also curious to see how it turned out. Napirai was a bit more sceptical about the whole business, understandably as she has no memory of those days and there's always the risk she could get the film mixed up with reality. I just keep praying that it will all work out and neither of us will regret it.

Through my collaboration with the filmmakers, however, I built up a few contacts in Kenya; and in December, completely spontaneously, I got the divorce papers out of the drawer again and faxed them to an acquaintance in Nairobi, asking him to discuss the case with a local lawyer. If ever there was a chance of an easy way to have my divorce recognized in Kenya, then this would be it, when we were in touch with the right people on the ground. With nothing to lose, I sat and waited for a reply.

My reading tour at the start of the new year kept me very busy. Reading about my exploits to hundreds of eager listeners and seeing the happy and amazed expressions on their faces is a real treat for me and I'm forever delighted by how many people say they get something out of it of relevance for their own lives. It has almost become like a vocation to me.

But precisely because I was so happy and satisfied with my work, I left it too late to realize that a domestic disaster had crept up on me while I wasn't looking. Ever so gradually, the man I had been sharing my life with had drifted out of it. By the time I had noticed what was happening it was already too late. I was both angry and upset at the same time, but I neither can nor want to talk about it anymore. Once again something had unexpectedly fallen apart at the seams. Now I realized that, even with all the love in the world, my new found fame has made life impossible for any man at my side. After the release of the film it could only get worse.

Nonetheless, I was not about to give up my way of life. I had fallen in love with a writing career that has allowed me to do good both here and in Africa. The huge number of letters I have received has proved to me that my books have helped countless people to overcome racial prejudice. Is there any higher calling, particularly when I myself am the mother to a mixed-race child? One thing was clear to me: from now on I would use my fame and all my energy for good. It was a decision that, once made, helped me to put the trauma of my failed relationship into perspective.

I plunged back into work, spending what free time I had with my daughter or going for long walks in the mountains I love so much. Then a few weeks later I got a message from Nairobi to say my European divorce papers were also legally valid in Kenya and that in Kenyan law there was also no question of having abducted my daughter fourteen years ago as her father had given his consent at the time to her leaving the country, even if he had not realized it might be for ever. I felt a great wave of relief wash over me, a kind of liberation.

Even so, I found that the effects of the collapse of my relationship were still taking their toll at night. I was having trouble sleeping and dreaming too much. Once I woke up in the middle of the night, sitting there bolt upright, covered in sweat, convinced that if I didn't go back to Kenya I'd never see my mother-in-law alive again. I spent the rest of the night tossing and turning and couldn't get back to sleep.

But the thought had implanted itself in my brain. Over the next few days I plagued myself with the question of whether or not I really should go back to Kenya. What would Napirai say? What about my mother? Apart from anything else, what would my African family think, above all Lketinga?

But the idea had taken hold of me, even though I kept experiencing radical mood swings. If I had still been with my partner, there would have been no question of going back to Kenya!

How strange was that? As if life really was predetermined and there was no avoiding fate.

I decided to go to Munich again to meet the director of the *White Masai* film who had meanwhile been to Kenya and met my family in Barsaloi. She said that after a certain initial wariness, she had been treated well and that eventually had even got to meet my mother-in-law. Mama was an old lady now, but still impressive. She had told her to tell me: 'Corinne should live to be ninety years old, just like me. She should know that I love her with all my heart, that she is welcome here whenever she wishes and that I would love to see her again before I die'.

When I heard these words, my eyes filled with tears. I suddenly felt intense empathy with the old lady and in that moment I made my decision: I had to see my mother-in-law again and hold her in my arms. I was going back to Africa.

I discussed it with my publishers. Albert, my editor, who had already been to see my family and taken them a copy of the first book, *The White Masai*, said he would be happy to come with me. 'That way I'll get to meet Little Albert,' he said with a smile. James, my ex-husband's brother, had actually named his own first son after him, as a gesture of thanks for the publishing house's generosity.

It was up to me now to tell James what I planned. He has been the link to the rest of the family, not least because he's the only one who can read and write. But I was tense and nervous as I waited for his reply. Then at the end of May the long-awaited letter arrived telling me how happy he and the rest of the family would be to see me. He said that Mama claimed she had always known that one day she would see me again. She was delighted and even Lketinga had said he wouldn't make trouble. According to James, everybody he told could hardly believe it and said: 'Really, Corinne will come once again to our place in Kenya?'

When I read the letter to my daughter she said off the top of her head: 'You know, Mum, you're right: you really do have to go back.' Those were the words I had been praying for, the words I needed. I love my daughter a lot and hoped I would return home with loads of new impressions, stories and photographs to share with her.

For four months I had agonized over whether or not going back was the right thing to do, whether everybody would come out of it okay, but now I was certain. I was certain that everything that had happened since the start of the year was planned to lead up to this reunion.

Nairobi

As we get off the plane, the air that greets us is not the moist tropical air that had first hit me back then in Mombasa. The air here is hot and dry. As we line up in queues for passport control I can't get rid of the queasy sensation in my stomach. I can't help but think back to how this was the point where, fourteen years ago, it all nearly went wrong for my daughter and me. I was all but sweating blood as I was forced to answer all their questions: why are you leaving the country without your daughter's father? Where is your husband? Why doesn't your daughter have a Kenyan child's identity card when she was born here and her father is a Samburu? Is this really your daughter? Question upon question until I was nearly crazy. I could hardly believe my luck when I got on board the plane. And now here I am, handing my passport over once again to one of these officials. He gives me a friendly smile, but my heart is pounding.

At least this time my daughter isn't with me. I considered it too dangerous to bring her along as she is not yet an adult. Under Kenyan law she belongs to her father, and under my ex-husband's tribal law she in fact belongs to her grandmother, his mother. Then from the Samburu point of view, Napirai is the perfect age for marriage at fifteen . Even nowadays the girls get married horrendously young and then are grotesquely mutilated by the so-called 'female circumcision'. I was simply not willing to take the risk of anything like that even coming into question. In any case, Napirai had no wish as yet to see Kenya again. Obviously she asked about her father and about our family history, but she is also wary of what has become unknown territory for her.

The immigration official takes my passport and runs it over a computer scanner – progress has made inroads here too. Five seconds later he stamps it and with some relief I enter Kenya, along with my two companions.

We have booked a room in the Norfolk Hotel for the first night. It's a hotel with history: built in 1904 in country-house style, during the colonial era it was the fashionable place for rich white settlers, business folk and big game hunters. It must have seemed like an oasis in this wild untamed country. There are photographs of famous people such as Roosevelt and Hemingway all over the walls. The gardens are a sea of tropical vegetation but with old-fashioned horse-drawn carriages in the drive. It's the first time I've stayed in such a smart hotel in Nairobi and daren't even think what it might cost. Without doubt, one night here has to cost a month's wages for one of the staff.

In the old days when I had to come to Nairobi, which was always an ordeal, I would look for something in River Road. It wasn't the best part of town then and still isn't. Back then I would pay just four or five Swiss francs for a night's accommodation. If you're married to a Samburu warrior and have to earn your money locally, there's no question of handing out what has been so hard earned for an expensive place to lay your head.

This time around, however, I'm with Europeans and my publisher wants the trip to be relatively comfortable. He's not exactly in his twenties anymore, nor has he fallen head over heels for a Masai woman.

We have dinner in the evening on the terrace. Behind us is the bar, to which the gentlemen used to withdraw with their cigars and was strictly off-limits to the ladies. None of this feels like Africa to me, even if there are more black business folk eating here than there would have been a few years ago. Apart from anything else, once my initial curiosity has worn off, it's all a bit too sophisticated and makes me want to get on with the trip. I have no regrets therefore when we press a tip into the white-gloved hand of the doorman in his bottle-green uniform and take our leave with a smile.

The Road to Samburu Country

We pick up two rented Land Cruisers with drivers and finally head off to my 'old home'. First we have to fight our way through the traffic chaos of Nairobi: a heaving throng of cars, lorries, the people-carrier taxis called *matatus* and the brightly coloured stinking long distance buses. Black clouds of exhaust smoke almost suffocate us. At the same time I'm fascinated once again by the way everybody is out to earn a couple of shillings. The newspaper sellers stand by the side of the road ready to weave amongst the lines of cars as soon as they come to a standstill. Somebody else is squeezing his way between the traffic trying to sell watches, torches and caps. I fancy one of his red head coverings and roll down the window to bargain with him. The salespeople rarely have enough time. We quickly agree on a price but he has no change and the traffic behind is pushing forward so we drive off. But our hawker isn't about to let a sale go that easily. In the rear-view mirror I can see the young lad running after us with giant strides. We've probably gone some 1,300 feet before a roundabout gives us another chance to stop. We've scarcely come to a stop when the hawker is by our window beaming in at us. In astonishment I buy my hat and our driver takes another one. That makes the smile grow even wider. I wish some of the salespeople back home in Switzerland could see someone as happy as this. We don't have people running after customers amidst the stench of exhaust fumes, but sometimes even so it takes little short of a miracle to get a friendly smile from some of our salespeople.

Fruit sellers with small piles of tomatoes, carrots, onions or bananas sit behind little wooden counters or by the side of the road, trying to sell their wares. Life in Nairobi is bright and colourful and despite the vast numbers of people it doesn't seem so hectic to me as a European city.

Eventually we get outside the city centre and now the effects of so-called progress are much more in evidence. Everywhere there are new supermarkets and businesses. Advertising hoardings for televisions, mobile phones and the latest films dominate the highway. Right by the side of the road there are beds and wardrobes for sale on display, with the occasional goat wandering amongst them grazing on bin rubbish or banana skins instead of grass. Laughing children in blue school uniforms troop along the roadside. But on the outskirts of the city a sea of corrugated iron roofs is still evidence of a huge and sprawling shantytown where the poorest of the poor live.

Our drivers have to be careful because the state of the roads, even here in Nairobi the capital, is catastrophic. We jolt through one pothole after another and in parts the road is completely unsurfaced. Every time we pick up speed we find traffic coming towards us on our side of the road. As a result the 105-mile journey to Nyahururu takes nearly five hours, although we have also taken a winding detour via Naivasha in order to get a view of the magnificent Rift Valley.

The Great Rift Valley – nicknamed the 'great ditch' – stretches several thousand miles through Africa: a great tear in the earth created millions of years ago when unimaginable subterranean forces pulled the plates of the earth's crust apart and the land between them sank. As a result, the land frequently drops away in breathtaking cliffs and vast gorges.

Standing on a not altogether reliable-looking extending wooden platform built for the large numbers of tourists I have a spectacular view of the vast plain and the mountain range in the distance. Directly beneath my feet is the thick deciduous forest that gradually thins out in the distance to a few thorn acacia trees and the red ochre earth. Looking at this view I get the first feeling that this really is home. At last this is something I recognize of the Kenya I love. The colour of the earth, the shapes of the trees and the sensation of overwhelming space reminds me of Barsaloi and a wave of happiness washes over me, pulling me onwards. But we still have a long way to travel before we reach my African home.

It is evening by the time we get to Nyahururu, which at 8,081 feet above sea level is the highest city in Kenya. On the right hand side of the street I recognize the old lodging house we used to use, the Nyahururu Space Haven

Hotel, although the blue-painted façade is now pink. It's immediately opposite the bus station so it's incredibly busy around now. Minibus drivers parp their horns to attract customers. This is a major transport hub. Arriving here from Maralal used to be like reaching the first outpost in Kenya of the 'big wide world'. Spending the night in Nyahururu on the way back from Nairobi was for me always a milestone marking the end of civilization, though I was always happy because I knew that in just sixteen miles I would be in Samburu country, my African family's homeland.

I absolutely have to go into the bus station to try to find the old bus I used to take. The appearance of three white people with photographic equipment and video cameras immediately creates a stir and we're surrounded by people asking questions or trying to sell things. I ask after the brightly painted old Maralal bus and am disappointed to be told that only *matatus* make the journey nowadays. It's a shame because I had imagined myself getting on that very bus next morning for the four-hour trip to Maralal just like in the old days. Even the process of loading up the bus used to fascinate me: the way they packed tables, cupboards, mattresses, water containers, boxes and other random possessions inside and on top of the bus. Now and then there would be an extra frisson to find the first few brightly decorated warriors with their long red hair mixing with the other passengers.

That was what I had been looking forward to: arriving in Maralal along with a jolly bunch of locals. Every trip was an adventure, not even knowing if we'd get there. How often had I sat there in the dirt by the side of the road out in the wilderness, the only white woman amongst all the Africans, stranded because our bus had got stuck in the mud? We would cut down branches from the shrubs to lay under the wheels until they could get purchase on them and we could get going again.

Such a pity that the bus, which has so many memories for me, is no longer there. Like it or lump it, I would have to make the journey in the comparative comfort of our Land Cruiser. With a last look around the square we set off to Thomson's Falls Lodging, where white people normally stay around here. It is an unpretentious but well-appointed lodging house, and as soon as we reach the entrance women from the souvenir shops are already swarming around us: 'Jambo, customer, how are you? I'm Esther. Come to my shop!' More women join in, all trying to impress their name upon us to make sure we go to the right shop tomorrow and buy the right thing. Their problem is that tomorrow is Sunday and therefore from nine in the morning until three in the afternoon they will be in church, so they want us to wait so as not to disappoint them. I'm afraid there's no chance of that: I have a family in Barsaloi who've already been waiting for fourteen years.

Before our departure we go to see Thomson's Falls, the famous 236-feet high waterfall. It's funny that I've done this trip so many times and until now never thought to stop and see the tourist sights.

After our visit to the waterfall we manage to escape relatively easily as the women have locked up the souvenir shops. This is where it really begins to get interesting for me as our destination for today is Maralal and if everything works out as planned, James will be waiting for us there. In his last letter he suggested he might come part of the way to meet us to show us the new road to Barsaloi.

I'm really looking forward to seeing him again and curious to know what news he'll have. Above all, I'd like to know how Lketinga feels about my visit. Is he happy about it or are there likely to be problems? Even though he has since married a native girl, I'm certain he still regards me as his wife. I've simply no idea how he's likely to react. I hope we manage to find James okay and he can reassure me.

We start out on an asphalt-surfaced road that goes as far as a little village called Rumuruti before turning into a rough track. From now on we're in Samburu country. All of a sudden the vegetation is different, as if there was a line drawn by a ruler across the landscape. Up until now we've been travelling through mostly green agricultural or meadow land, but from here on the land is arid and the colour of the earth begins to change from beige to red. The temperature rises too.

There are no more tarmac roads here, just rough tracks. Our vehicles leave a huge cloud of dust behind us and we're getting shaken to the bone. When my companion comments on the state of the road I can assure him with a laugh that fourteen years ago it was much worse. The bumpy ride cheers me up and I get happier by the moment. I have incredibly vivid memories of this road and all the hazards along it and I ask the driver to let me take the wheel.

If I can't travel this road on the big old bus then I'd at least like to remind myself of my beaten-up old Land Rover. We bounce along the road and I have to really concentrate to make sure we avoid the biggest potholes at least.

From the corner of my eye, however, I can't help noticing the first *manyattas* some distance from the road. Every now and then a few white goats pop up in front of the car. They're slow to get out of the road, and the eyes of the children minding them follow us. Most of the boys carry a stick horizontally behind their back in the crook of their elbows. The little girls, on the other hand, laugh and wave at the white '*mzungus*'. After two hours we come to a little village, identifiable only by a couple of shops on either side of the road and a group of people in brightly coloured clothing standing in front of them. No, there is one more thing that indicates human habitation that we didn't have earlier: plastic! It is tragic to see how much inroad plastic has made into Kenya. Fifteen hundred feet before each village the first signs of it appear: starting with just pink, blue or clear plastic bags hanging on the shrubs, but then the nearer we get the worse it is. There are plastic bottles impaled on virtually every thorn on every bush. At first glance it almost looks like they're in bloom, but a second later the tragic truth is all too painfully evident. When I was living in Kenya there was virtually no plastic here. If someone got hold of a plastic bag from a tourist, they would have looked after it as if it were something precious and used it again and again. Now they hang on the bushes in their thousands.

Maralal

Shortly before we reach our destination for the day I hand the wheel back to our driver so I can properly take everything in as we drive into Maralal. It's soon clear how much the town has grown. There are new roads, although still unsurfaced, even a roundabout, and directly opposite it – I can hardly believe my eyes – a new BP service station with a shop, just like we have back in Europe. Before long I realize that Maralal nowadays has three filling stations, and petrol is available all the time. It was so different in my day. I never knew when the solitary petrol station would get a delivery of fuel. Sometimes we had to wait for more than a week and then drive back on the dangerous bush track carrying a full forty-gallon canister. When we got home I had to decide where to store it, given that there were always fires in and around the *manyattas*. Thank God Father Giuliani helped out, letting us store it in the Mission. The filling stations today are obviously a godsend to everyone who has a car. But then back then there were no more than ten cars in the whole district.

We drive slowly in our Land Cruisers past the market, which hasn't changed much. There are still lots of wooden stalls next to one another with colourful pretty Masai blankets and cloth waving in the wind. Behind, as ever, is the post office. Only later do I find out, to my astonishment, that it contains four computers that people from the Mission and former schoolchildren can use to access the internet and the wider world.

We drive as slowly as possible, looking out for James. I suggest we drive once around the whole town, as a group of white people will stand out and James will be sure to hear of our arrival.

The centre of Maralal is unchanged despite the fact that the town has grown in all directions. We pass my Italian friend Sophia's little house and memories of her come flooding back. She was a good friend to me back then. We were lucky enough to both be pregnant at the same time and give birth to our daughters the same week. We were the first white women to have children in this area and were able to share a room in the hospital in Wamba. It was thanks to Sophia and her Italian cooking that I was able to put on the 22 pounds I needed in the last month of pregnancy to reach the 150 pounds that was considered the minimum weight for giving birth. Nowadays, at five foot nine, I weigh substantially more even when not in the ninth month of pregnancy. How I wish I could see Sophia and her daughter again!

When we've done our tour of the town we park in front of the lodging house where I used to spend the night with Lketinga. No sooner have we got out of the cars than we're surrounded by at least eight young men trying to sell us things. One of them tells us that just a few weeks ago, here in this very lodging house, they were making a film, called *The White Masai*. He asks if we've ever heard of it. One of the others nods in agreement and asks if we're part of the film crew. We say no to everything and go on into the restaurant.

The décor is different to how I remember it. The centre of the room is dominated by a bar counter with a wire grille in front of it. We get a cola passed through. The young men from outside have piled in after us, a few of them smelling of beer. One of them asks me my name and I give one at random. I don't want to declare myself to be the original 'white Masai' not least because I have no idea how welcome the film crew were in Maralal. On the other hand, what if James were to walk in at any moment?

To change the subject I ask if there are any samosas to be had. Immediately one of the men runs off and come back in a few minutes to lay ten samosas wrapped in old newspaper on the table. I wolf down three of them happily. My companions Albert and Klaus, however, seem to lose their appetite at the sight of the printer's ink soaked in fat.

But what about James? After half an hour he still hasn't turned up. What if he didn't get my last letter? Not that I specified an exact meeting place. Maralal was clear enough in my memory.

Meanwhile the samosas on the table have been joined by a mountain of tourist souvenirs, handmade Masai jewellery, little wooden headrests and even *rungus* – the warrior's fighting clubs. The atmosphere, however, is getting less comfortable. We pay up, an enormous sum in local terms, for the samosas and leave the remainder to the other guests. Outside there's still no sign of James so we decide to drive up to the Safari Lodge to check in to our rooms.

I have very specific memories of this Lodge. I sat out on the terrace here the first time I came to Maralal looking for my husband-to-be. For hours on end I watched zebras, apes and wild boar around the waterhole, wondering behind which of these surrounding hills my hard-to-find warrior lived and whether he knew I was nearby. Armed with a handful of photographs I wandered around Maralal every day asking travellers in traditional dress if they knew Lketinga. It was ten days before my efforts were rewarded and my prayers answered. At last I was able to throw my arms around the great love of my life and let our destiny take its course.

Later my then husband would bring me back to this Lodge when I was so weak with malaria that I could hardly stand. I had kept no food down for weeks and Lketinga in his despair had brought me to the one place he knew where there were salads and sandwiches – white people's food. And indeed, after months of maize porridge and goat meat it took nothing more than a simple ham and cheese salad sandwich to give me a new lease of life.

Up until now, however, I had never spent a night here.

Reunion With James

I shake myself out of my daydreams and walk down to the car to fetch my luggage. Suddenly there's the growl of an engine and a motorbike comes roaring up and immediately – although I can hardly believe it – I realize it's James! He can ride a motorbike! Carefully he parks the little all-terrain bike on one side, takes his hat off and, dressed in a thick jacket despite the heat, runs across to me with outstretched arms like a little boy. We throw our arms around each other in sheer delight.

For all these years the only contact we have had with one another has been by letter. He is my link to the rest of the family. For a while we can do nothing but laugh together. I'm astounded at how James has grown up. Last time I saw him he was a schoolboy of about seventeen; now he's a mature man.

James is just as effusive in greeting Albert, my publisher, whom he already knows, and Klaus. He tells us animatedly that he just spotted our cars as we were leaving Maralal and fetched the motorbike to catch up with us. We're amazed we didn't see him in the rear-view mirror, but then the cars were kicking up such a cloud of dust, and then again, we weren't expecting to see him on a motorbike.

After we've got over the excitement of seeing one another again we all go across to sit on the terrace and talk. James is now taller than I am and his face has filled out, which makes his eyes appear smaller than they used to be. He's very fit and wearing warm clothing including good stout shoes, a type of walking boot I've never seen around here before. Most of the locals used to wander around in sandals made out of old car tyres or plastic flip-flops.

With a big smile he tells us the whole of Barsaloi is excited about our arrival and that Mama won't believe it until we're standing outside her *manyatta*. She is delighted and keeps saying she always knew she would see me again. Albert asks him about the motorbike and James's eyes light up. He's very proud that only he and one old friend from school have managed to learn to ride a motorbike. It makes things vastly easier for him to be able to use it on the long journey between his school and his family. Unfortunately he can only afford to use it at weekends as otherwise the costs in petrol and upkeep are too high. He is the headmaster of a small school a few miles beyond Barsaloi and the journey takes forty-five minutes. It's hard to believe that a head teacher can't afford to drive home on his motorbike every night, but that's northern Kenya – Samburu country – and as far as James is concerned it's normal enough. He's happy enough to actually own a motorbike.

Obviously I have to give him news of Napirai. Why did she not come with me? How big is she now? Does she ask after her African family? Is she going to come and see them one day? Does she like school? Question after question, and I do my best to answer them all. I tell James the truth, that I want to get a first impression myself, to bring back photographs and some video to inspire Napirai to come and visit. If everything goes well, she'll definitely be with me next time.

The time flies by and before we know it we're all being called in to dinner. We're the Lodge's only guests. Even back in the old days I never ran across any other tourists here but somehow it still manages to function. This is the first time James has been here and he's interested to see how they lay out the cutlery on either side of the plate.

The starter is toast with mushrooms and I have to laugh because I know the Samburu don't eat mushrooms. James asks cautiously what sort of a dish it is, looking rather embarrassedly at the little piece of toast. I'm laughing so much I can hardly explain to him. All the time I can hear Lketinga's words: 'White people's food is not proper food, you will never be full by eating it.' He would make exactly the same face that James is making now. Eventually I pull myself together and tell him what it is, and that it's only a starter. 'Okay,' he says, 'No problem. I'll try it. I'm a guest after all, and a guest should eat what's put in front of him.'

After a few minutes, however, I rescue James from his toast as the second course – a tomato soup – is already being served. He finds that somewhat better although still unusual. And then at least a piece of meat arrives. At last that's something he understands even if it is a bit small by his standards. But there's nothing I can do to persuade him to touch the last course – a wholly alien chocolate mousse.

Throughout the meal we're all talking and laughing and I ask tentatively about Lketinga. James replies: 'He is not bad in this time.' It seems things are going okay for him and a month ago he married a second young girl. I'm surprised as nobody mentioned this in any of the recent letters. James explains that Lketinga only decided on another marriage recently. His first wife – or second after me, depending on your point of view – is sickly and has had a number of miscarriages. Until now Lketinga has only one daughter in Kenya, Shankayon, and he would like more children, having waited long enough for them. His sick wife left Barsaloi a few months ago to go back to her mother.

This is all unexpected news to me, and a bit disconcerting: I hope my turning up doesn't cause any extra difficulties. But when I tell James of my fears, he smiles and says: 'No, no, there won't be any problems.'

He says that Lketinga didn't want to be without a wife by his side when I arrived as this might have given me the wrong impression. And as he wants more children anyhow, it's all for the best. I find the first part of this a bit much but am still pleased that Lketinga has a wife from his own tribe at his side. She's probably a young girl not much older than our daughter Napirai!

It may be hard to imagine for us Europeans but in Samburu culture there's no real alternative for the men but to choose young brides. Girls are often married off to men up to forty years older than them and when they die their wives are not allowed to remarry. They may still have children but they are given the name of the widow's late husband and never told who their real father is. Marriage for love is relatively unknown among the Samburu. Lketinga and I were a major exception to the rule. I know that he found that something strange and wonderful but at the same time confusing and unsettling.

I'm fascinated to know how things with his new wife came about. I knew the other wife when she came into our shop as a girl to buy food. Years later I was delighted to spot her again on the video that Father Giuliani took during our marriage ceremony. I would have liked to meet her again as a young woman and the mother of Napirai's half-sister.

We go inside from the terrace for a last glass of wine. James sticks to Coke as he isn't used to wine and anyway has to get back to Maralal on the motorbike. Gazing into a flickering fire I listen attentively to James telling Albert and Klaus about the first time he met me. It was outside the school in Maralal just after I had finally found Lketinga. He took me down to the school to meet his little brother and to tell him that we were off to Mombasa together. James, who was about fourteen at the time, had to be fetched out of class and was very shy, coming over with his head down, scarcely daring to look up at us.

And now here he is trying to describe what he felt back then: 'I was very unsure of myself because I thought this white lady was my sponsor. I knew that an American lady financed our school and couldn't understand what she was doing standing there in front of me. What did it all mean? I was very nervous. It was only when my brother told me Corinne belonged to him and had come here to find him that I realized what was what.

'But even that seemed crazy to me. My brother with a white woman who wanted to come and live with our Mama? I could see problems ahead: my big brother had never been to school and knew nothing at all about the white people's world. Everybody else back home too knew only the traditional Samburu way of life. It was different for me because I'd been to school and I could see only problems ahead.

'Lketinga is older than I am. He was a warrior while I was just an uncircumcised schoolboy. I could hardly tell a warrior what I thought. The problems began back in Mombasa already and just a few weeks later there was Corinne standing outside the school again, alone this time, once again looking for my brother, who was by this stage not well in the head. She asked me to take her back to my family in Barsaloi.

'I said I'd help even though it was going to cause a lot of problems just to get out of school for a couple of days. We're normally only allowed out of school during the holidays or when someone back home has died. It really wasn't easy. Thank God she eventually found another alternative and got there on her own.'

And he looks across at me and laughs. Much of what he's just told us has given me a whole new perspective on the turn of events back then, while at the same time bringing it all sharply back into focus.

Tomorrow morning it will be time to take the biggest step of all, the last leg of the journey, from Maralal to Barsaloi and my first meeting with Lketinga since I fled from him fourteen years ago. I can't help feeling uneasy. The fire in the lodge hearth has burned low now, and we're all feeling tired and drained from the long journey and the initial excitement of meeting up. We agree to meet James early in morning outside the post office to go shopping together for essentials.

We retire to our rooms and I'm pleased to find a small fire burning in the hearth here too. Before long I'm in bed under the mosquito net waiting for sleep to take me. But as everything goes quiet I'm only too aware how wound up I am inside. Instead of sleep all that comes to me is a deep feeling of sadness. The more I think about it the more certain I am that when I see Mama and Lketinga tomorrow I'll burst into tears, and that would be a terrible *faux pas* in Samburu eyes. Tears are reserved for bereavement.

I get up again and sit outside on the doorstep soaking in the night-time tranquillity. It's almost a full moon. Strange noises emanate from the bush but I can see nothing. Then comes the nearby growl of a great ape and suddenly in the distance I can hear the singing of Samburu warriors. Somewhere out there dozens of warriors and girls have gathered to dance in the moonlight. In the wind the sound of their singing dips and rises, and in between I can clearly hear the stamping of feet, now and again interrupted by a short sharp cry. I sit there remembering how these beautifully decorated young men would leap into the air while the young girls would bob their heads and their heavy necklaces in time. I used to watch my husband dance like that and every time it never failed to excite and move me.

The sadness and the sense of uncertainty have faded now and I feel happy and free. I'm ready now to meet the family tomorrow and can even look forward to it. At peace with the world again I crawl back beneath the mosquito netting, sniff the sweet smoke from the fire and fall fast asleep.

We meet up next morning at the post office as arranged and are immediately surrounded by the same young men as yesterday still keen to test their marketing skills. To our surprise someone gives Albert, who we have told them – to spare me any hassle – is my father, a traditional hardwood *rungu* club.

But it's not until James has had a few words with the youths that we're left to go round the market more or less in peace to find a nice warm blanket for my mother-in-law. I have two other blankets in my luggage, an orange-red one for Lketinga because I know he likes this colour, and a checked one for his older brother. The Samburu men wear them as warm clothing. For Mama we buy a good thick wool blanket.

Then we take the cars to a wholesale food store and order a 55-pound sack of rice and the same of good quality maize meal, as well as various cooking fats, powdered tea, sweets, soap and other bits and bobs. At the same time we order up several pounds of tomatoes, carrots, cabbage, onions and oranges. We have to take something for ourselves too unless we want to live on goat meat.

Just before we leave, James runs across to the tobacco shop to pick up six pounds of chewing tobacco, which for the old folk is almost more important than food. A woman dressed beautifully in traditional clothes climbs into one of the cars with us, delighted to be given the chance to get a lift for the long journey. It goes without saying here that if there is a spare seat in a car someone must fill it.

From Maralal to Barsaloi

At last we're on the road. James is leading the way on his motorbike. There's a new road because the old one is now definitively impassable. It's a pity as I'd like to have shown it to my companions. The new one was just finished a few months ago and makes for a relatively easy ride. For the past few years they've had to put up with a five-hour detour by way of Baragoi.

Soon we leave the last few mud holes and puddles of rainwater behind us as the road starts to climb mercilessly. James's motorbike kicks out a thick cloud of black smoke. A few people on foot pass us coming the other way towards town, the woman carrying calabash gourds filled with milk to sell. Every day they walk hours in each direction in order to make a small profit.

The hollowed-out calabash gourds are light and have been used as containers since prehistoric times. The Masai and Samburu use strips of leather decorated with coloured beads or little shells to strengthen them. To keep them reusable the women scour the interior every night with a red-hot firebrand that sterilizes them. That's why the milk usually smells a bit smoky, but back in Mama's hut it always tasted wonderful to me.

The men are usually pulling one or more goats behind them, sometimes even a cow, taking them to market in Maralal. They only part with animals when they urgently need money for ritual celebrations, weddings or hospital bills.

Even when our driver has to engage the four-wheel drive this is a much more comfortable way to travel than the old bush road. There are no elephants or buffalo breaking suddenly out of the jungle to bar our path. After an hour or so of driving up hill and down dale we get to a small *manyatta* village called Opiroi. A few women sitting outside the huts with their children look at our cars while the little kids, either naked or wearing just T-shirts, wave from the side of the road.

The little square is dominated by a half-finished church. We press on, however, because we want to get to Barsaloi as quickly as possible. Every now and then we drive across the dried-up beds of little streams; water is still scarce here.

To my astonishment we come across a herd of camels, frightened by the noise of our engines, charging off as if in slow motion into the bush. It would appear the Samburu have taken to keeping more of these animals.

At last we reach a high pass between two rocky hills and know that from here on the cloud of dust we kick up will be visible in Barsaloi, even though the village is still half an hour's drive away. No doubt today the whole village is out waiting for us.

When we pause briefly Klaus suggests he goes ahead with one of the drivers in order to get good footage of my arrival and reunion. James agrees and says he'll try to explain this to Lketinga. In the meantime Albert and I can take a look at the school down by the Barsaloi River. It was just being built when I left the village and there was nothing more than a few walls to see. Even today, we are soon to discover, there's an awful lot lacking, but at least the local children have their own school.

Just as Klaus is leaving, however, my old uneasy feeling comes creeping back. What will Lketinga say when the first person he sees is someone he doesn't know carrying a video camera? And what about the other people in the village? What will they make of it? Most of them have never even seen a film and don't understand the concept. And Klaus wants to erect a tripod!

Despite my dreadful unease about the whole business, the thought of Napirai calms me down. After all, I want to capture as much as I can of the trip for her sake. This is the first time her parents have met in years. She has no memory of her time in Kenya and it all seems a bit strange to her. She's caught between two cultures but actually only lives in one. My heart hankers more after Africa than hers does. She thinks like a white European but isn't seen as one. It's not easy for her and that's why I want to bring back as much as possible in pictures and video so she can get an idea of her African family.

Even so, the nervous tension and feeling of uneasy anticipation has built up to almost unbearable levels by the time I make out in the distance the first houses of Barsaloi. It looks as if the village has grown a bit, but the sight is still so familiar that I feel I could have been here the day before yesterday.

The long low building of the school peeks out behind the shrubs and thorn trees. We drive slowly up to a gate where the head teacher is waiting to welcome us. The wall behind him is decorated with various murals, one showing a judge in his robes, another two children playing football while a third depicts a well-dressed man working at a computer on a desk. Above them is the inscription: 'Walk out productive'. Out here so far from anywhere the image of the computer still comes across as comic, especially when we know from James that there's often a shortage of paper and pens. Even he has no idea about computers.

The headmaster takes us around the school and I'm quite amazed how much they've achieved with the few means at their disposal. The classrooms are simple but well fitted out. The windows have wire grilles rather than glass. The headmaster's pride and joy is the library with a few books. The children can come and fetch a book, which they can read in the rather spartan reading room. They aren't allowed to take them home, however, because the smoke in the *manyattas* would damage them.

A few children are looking curiously through the grilles at their white visitors. In one corner of the playground others are lined up to have *ugali*, a sort of maize porridge, served on aluminium trays. I'm sure they're all proud that their parents even send them to school, and I can't help wondering what my daughter would think if she had to go to school here.

At last we drive gently down the steep bank of the Barsaloi River and cross the five hundred feet of dried-up river bed. A few yards more and we'll be there. Already I can see the first huts on either side of the road.

My heart is pounding as I try to take in as much as possible at once. Where will Lketinga be? Where will he greet me? Is he going to be in the middle of the village or in one of the huts, away from all the inquisitive eyes? There are so many new wooden huts that I don't know where I should be looking. There are people everywhere. Ahead on the left I spot the Mission building. It looks smaller than it used to. The green banana trees are gone too. The church is finished, however. Children jump out of the road as our car passes by.

There they are! At last I spot our other vehicle and James's motorbike. Our driver stops next to them. As I rather uncertainly go to get out suddenly two arms shoot through the open car window and grab me by the neck and I feel kisses all over my face and hear over and over again: 'Oh, Corinne, oh, Corinne!' I have no idea what's going on, let alone who it is that's hanging round my neck. James hurries up and guides the obviously emotional man away. One thing's for sure: it certainly wasn't Lketinga!

Lketinga

At last I manage to get out and can see around me. There, some sixty feet away, in the shade of a leafy thorn tree, I spot Lketinga. Tall and proud, he's standing with one leg elegantly crossed over the other, the typical pose of the Masai.

I know there's no way he'll move an inch. It is simply not done for a traditional Samburu to come to a woman. So, with the eager eyes of the surrounding crowd watching, I walk up to him. There isn't a thought in my head. I can't think anymore. The only thing I'm aware of is the throbbing beat of my heart. Each step seems like a hundred.

Lketinga is every bit as tall and slim as ever. He has one hand on his hip, while he leans elegantly with the other on a tall stick. He is wearing a red loincloth with a yellow T-shirt and a white shawl with blue spots across his shoulders. As ever, his feet are clad in sandals made of old car tyres. In the hand resting on the stick he also carries his *rungu*, while from beneath his T-shirt on his right side protrudes the red leather sheath of his bush knife.

My eyes take all this in even as I'm walking towards him, and at the same time I hear his slightly hoarse, soft, laughing voice call out to me: 'Hey, you are looking big, very big, like an old Mama.' With a welcome like that, all my shy embarrassment evaporates and I give as good back: 'And you look like an old man!'

And then I'm right up close to him, looking into his eyes, when everything happens of its own accord. We throw our arms around one another, and hold each other tight. Neither of us cares that the locals don't do things like that. We hadn't planned it; all of a sudden it just seems the right thing to do. After a few seconds I let go of Lketinga and look him in the face. We run our eyes over one another. He looks much better than he did six years ago when Albert met him in Maralal to give him a copy of *The White Masai*.

The picture he brought back with him had shocked me. Today, however, I can see in his face much of his old good looks. He still has his magnificent profile, fine features, not too big a nose and full, attractive lips. When he smiles his white teeth – with the gap in the middle – sparkle. His cheek bones stand out more strongly than ever, which creates the slight suggestion that his cheeks have sunken somewhat. There are a few wrinkles now on his high forehead but his crinkly hair is as almost as black as ever. In his ear lobes – stretched long, Samburu-style – are little silver metal rings.

As we're talking relaxedly to one another he suddenly grabs my right arm with its silver bangle holds it up and asks me in some confusion: 'What is this? Why are you not still wearing the bangle I gave you at our wedding? What sort of a bracelet is this and what does it mean?' A bit taken aback, I answer him slightly embarrassedly but with a laugh: 'You said yourself I'd got fatter. I had to have our bracelet cut off because it had got too tight for my arm.' But he doesn't understand and stands there shaking his head.

It's been an emotional few minutes and I realize tears are welling up in my eyes. Oh God, not now! I turn my face away from Lketinga to hide my emotion, but he grabs my arm again: 'Don't cry! Why are you crying? That's no good!' I take a deep breath, bite my lips and try to get a grip on myself. I can't collapse in floods of tears in front of all these people. Grown women don't cry here. To change the subject I ask after Mama. Lketinga nods and says: 'Okay, okay, I'll take you to Mama later. *Pole, pole* – slowly, slowly.'

It's only now that I notice Klaus, who's been filming everything all along. Albert comes across slowly and Lketinga greets him with a handshake and friendly smile. You can see how proud he is to have all these visitors. As ever he carries himself graciously, calmly and without rush. The only one who's in a dither is me. Even so, I'm amazed how simply and naturally I'm getting on with Lketinga, even playfully. It's as if all those years have rolled away. We've straight away gone back to using 'our' special language, a blend of simplistic English mixed with Masai words. Right from the start we've been teasing one another: 'Why have you dyed your hair red like a warrior?' he says. 'You really are an old Mama.' And he laughs and shakes his head.

Then all of a sudden his eyes go dark and I notice that threatening furrow between his eyebrows that always presaged something unpleasant. In a serious voice he asks: 'Where is my child? Why has my child not come with you?' My heart skips a beat and then starts pounding. I look him straight in the eyes and tell him Napirai has a lot of schoolwork to do at the moment. Later, when she's got all of that behind her, she'll almost certainly come to Barsaloi. He's watching me closely but then his face relaxes and he says: 'Okay, it's okay. I wait for my child. I really hope that she will come.'

Looking over towards a long building on one side, I notice Lketinga's older brother Papa Saguna sitting in the shade with the other men watching us. Glad to see him, I wave him over and he gets up and comes across. He is effectively head of the family as their father is dead, and as the eldest his word is usually taken as law. He speaks only Maa, which makes it difficult for me to communicate with him. But I'm relieved to see him smiling. In the old days I was never sure whether or not he liked me. In some ways he always seemed the wildest of the family to me. Whenever he spoke in his rough, coarse voice it always sounded as if he was looking for an argument. He came with us on our wedding trip to Mombasa to act as a witness and I will never forget his childlike amazement at life in the city. Here in the bush he's the toughest member of the family, but he was terrified by the sight of the ocean and the half-naked tourists in Mombasa. I'm really pleased he's here. Later on James tells me that despite having had a fever he walked for four hours from his village to be here when I arrived.

Lketinga leads us off to a well-kept corral, and once again I can't help being fascinated at the way this man moves. We walk towards a long, thin wooden house with a tin roof, which I discover to be the home of James and his family. From all around I hear people call: '*Supa, Mama Napirai. Serian a ge?* – Hello, Mama Napirai, how are you?'

We pass through the six-foot high thorn thicket that starts just outside the house and surrounds the whole family area like a fence, protecting them from wild animals. During the day they leave a narrow opening in it, which is closed up at night when they've brought the animals in.

Every few feet I have to shake hands and smile into different faces. Most of them are women. They all give me beaming smiles and apart from greeting me with the usual '*Supa*', ask if I remember them. I recognize a few straight away but there are others whom I can hardly recall at first. One old woman with only a couple of teeth left in her mouth comes up with a big smile and spits in my hands, as a way of giving me her blessing. She is the mother of a girl I visited in her hut just after she'd undergone so-called female circumcision. She was a neighbour of ours who was married at the age of twelve and, according to Samburu tradition, had to undergo this horrific ritual on the morning of her marriage. I want to ask the old woman how her daughter is because I remember her really well as a happy, laughing child, but I can't because the oldest people here understand only Maa and, apart from a few set phrases, I don't speak any. All of a sudden I feel really useless; there's so much I want to say and so little I can. It will be the same with Mama.

James urges me on. Within the corral there are three larger *manyattas* for living in and two little ones where the kid goats are kept during the day when their mothers are taken out to pasture. The newborns, however, are kept in the big *manyattas* with the humans. *Manyatta* walls are made of thin planks of wood placed tightly together and plastered with dried cow dung. The roof is made of goatskins, hand-woven sisal matting, old sacks and pieces of cardboard, all somehow interleaved to provide protection from the rain. Outside the door there's usually a rolled-up cowhide, a pile of firewood and oval willow wickerwork baskets which, if they need to up sticks and move, can be strapped on the back of a donkey and used to carry everything. Everything they have has to fit in there.

A few chickens are pecking in the red-brown sandy earth around the *manyattas*. I'm astonished to see all these birds because the Samburu have absolutely no tradition of keeping poultry. When I arrived with a chicken for the first time it caused a great stir. Nobody had a clue what to do with something that to them was a useless animal. They ate neither eggs nor chicken meat and the only thing Mama could see was the problem of preventing the wild animals getting it. She was also worried that it would attract birds of prey that would be a threat to the baby goats. And yet now there were at least ten chickens running around. When I expressed my astonishment to James, he grins and says: 'You showed us what could be done with these animals. My wife cooks with eggs every now and then and what we don't eat we sell in our little shop to the nuns from the Mission.' There's another piece of news: in Father Giuliani's day there were no nuns at the Mission.

Mama

James disturbs my train of thought to say: 'I'll show you around later. Right now let's go and say hello to Mama. This is her hut.' He's pointing to a hut about the height of an average person. I'm about to bend down and crawl through the little opening when James stops me and whispers: 'No, no, let Mama come out or else you won't be able to say hello properly with all that smoke in the little hut. And it's an excuse to get Mama to come out for once.'

He says a few words in Maa at the door and I hear her rattling around inside, bending down to crawl out of the *manyatta*. And then suddenly after fourteen years, she's standing there in front of me again. To my complete astonishment I realize that in all this time she's hardly changed at all. I had imagined her much older and weaker. Instead the Mama standing in front of me is a dignified and still imposing woman. We each reach out a hand and as they meet we look each other in the eyes silently, trying to say as much as we can without speaking.

My God, what an aura this woman projects! I do my best to read her emotions in her faintly clouded eyes. It's not the done thing in Samburu culture to throw your arms around each other and give vent to emotional outpourings. People try to suppress their strongest feelings and look as serious and unmoved as possible. We remain there clutching each other's hands for what seems like an eternity.

I'd love so much to be able to tell her how important it is to me to see her again, that for all these years I have lived in the hope of being able to come face to face with her again, that she has been in all my prayers, that she has been one of the most important figures in my emotional life. Instead, all I can do is stand there mute and do my best to convey what I feel with my eyes and my heart.

31

Suddenly she reaches out her right hand and touches my face, squeezes my chin tenderly and, smiling happily, whispers: 'Corinne, Corinne, Corinne!' Now the taboo has gone and I put my arms around her and can't stop myself planting a kiss on her grey head. At this moment I'm overwhelmed with happiness that I managed to find the courage to come back, and I get the impression that for her too it's a very emotional experience.

For a fleeting second my thoughts flash back to the first time we met, when I had finally found Lketinga after a long and adventurous search and the two of us were sitting on a cowhide in the *manyatta* talking merrily when the crouched form of Mama had appeared in her hut, sat down opposite us and stared at me in what seemed like stony disapproving silence, with the smoke from the fire rising between us. Just like today we probed one another with our eyes and tried to read the other's soul in her face. Back then she broke the ice by reaching out a hand to take mine, just as today she reached out to stroke my face.

Now all the pent-up tension and emotion of the two meetings subside and I simply start talking to hold back the tears. I compliment her on her appearance. She still has a full face with scarcely a wrinkle. At most she has simply become a little bit smaller and thinner. Her hair is cropped close and has gone grey, which only has the effect of making her eyebrows look darker. Many Samburu have problems with their eyes because of the open fire in their *manyattas* and the smoke from them. She is wearing several layers of coloured bead necklaces around her neck and earrings of glass beads and brass. On her arms and feet I recognize the narrow silver bands she always wore, now digging deep into her flesh. They are like the jewellery Lketinga gave me at our wedding and I wore them until I began to get painful cuts on my ankles that wouldn't heal for months at a time. The scars are still there.

Mama's clothing is an old blue kanga thrown over her shoulders and a brown skirt stained in several places. I'm glad I have three new skirts for her in my luggage. James might have bought her a skirt from time to time from the money we sent him. But here they will wear a piece of clothing until it falls apart and the old people at least are of the opinion that you can only wear one at a time.

I move aside to let Albert pay his respects to Mama too. She remembers his last visit and is pleased to see him. Klaus, on the other hand, she regards with some suspicion. She doesn't know him and with his camera he looks potentially dangerous to her. James and Lketinga act as interpreters so we can have a conversation. I fetch the new blanket and hand it to her but instead of being pleased, a frown passes over her face. Somewhat disconcerted, I wonder what it is she doesn't like. Only later do I discover that she doesn't approve of other people seeing what presents she gets, because it can cause envy and suchlike problems.

To put her in a better mood I rummage in my rucksack and produce the little album of photos of Napirai that I've put together for Lketinga and her. I've arranged them with the most recent photos at the front, so that the further back it goes, the younger Napirai gets. Immediately Mama and Lketinga sit down together and start looking at the pictures. Her father is amazed to see how big his daughter is and laughs: 'She's nearly as tall as I am.' Mama asks of every photo if it's still Napirai. Somehow all the different scenes, which I deliberately picked out, confuse her. But as we get to the younger photos of Napirai, she perks up more. By now there are nearly a dozen heads gathered around the little album. Everybody wants to see Napirai. Even Papa Saguna, Lketinga's big brother, is interested and now and then breaks out in a laugh displaying his faultless white teeth. When we get to the picture in which Napirai is photographed next to some of the family goats, quite a discussion breaks out. Then when we reach the very last pictures Mama reaches out her hand to stroke the photographs and says, 'Yes, now I recognize the little girl, my little Napirai,' and smiles happily at me. When we get to the final picture, she claps the album closed, shoves it under her kanga and thanks me with the words: '*Asche oleng*'.

One Big Family

Now it's James's turn to invite us into his home to introduce us to his family. His wife has made *chai*, the traditional very sweet tea with goat's milk. It's just twenty yards from Mama's *manyata* to his modest little house. A few children playing outside fall in behind us. At the doorway a pretty, plump young woman appears and he introduces her as his wife, Mama Saruni. Saruni, a hyperactive three-year-old, is their eldest daughter.

Married people amongst the Samburu are never referred to by their first names. If anyone does so by mistake they have to hand over a goat by way of recompense. First names are considered very personal. While a couple are still without children they call themselves '*mparatut*' – wife – and '*lepayian*' – husband. But as soon as a child is born everybody refers to them as Mama or Papa and then the name of the child. It's only considered acceptable to use someone's name when they aren't physically present. Strangers are addressed by their family name and the names of their father and mother.

All these complicated customs with names cause me some embarrassment as to what I should call Lketinga. In the old days I always called him 'darling' which would be more than a little out of place now. But nor do I want to call him '*lepayian*' – husband – as I've divorced him and I don't want to give him false expectations. 'Papa Napirai' is a possibility but I can't bring myself to say it. It's going to be hard to start a conversation with him from two or three yards' distance. One way or another we're going to have to either go over to one another, catch each other's eye or prod one another on the arm to get their attention to speak to them.

My first impression of James's wife is rather good. Superficially I wouldn't have taken her for a Samburu. Like James she's been to school, and instead of traditional tribal jewellery she's wearing a fashionable fine necklace of black and gold beads. Also she hasn't shaved her head as most women here do but has covered it with a rather original and fashionably arranged headscarf. She's dressed in modern style with a knitted twin-set and a dark red skirt. It's as if James and she live in a different century to the rest of the family. She's carrying her youngest baby on one arm and shakes hands with the other. But despite her modern appearance she seems shy, speaking softly and only meeting our eyes briefly.

We go in to the living room, which is spacious and furnished with simple wooden chairs, tables and stools. The wall decoration, however, is to say the least, eclectic. Next to two wedding photos in which James is dressed as a traditional warrior is a picture of him in a dark suit and tie. What a contrast! A picture of some Kenyan ministers, a giant poster of the Brazilian football team and a teddy bear hanging on a nail next to a Christian cross create a collage of contrasts that makes me smile to myself. Seen from a central European point of view it all seems rather spartan and yet slightly comic, yet when I recall our life in the *manyatta* it has to be seen as baronial.

I sit down on one of the stools with Lketinga on the other side of the table. He crosses his long legs and wraps one of his hands around the thin stick he never goes anywhere without. It is sort of a substitute spear. His whole bearing is at once dignified and yet somehow feminine. I'm delighted to see him in such good shape because, after all, he's still the father of my daughter and I want her to be proud of him. He watches me constantly.

I let my eyes wander around the room while James's wife fetches enamel teacups and Thermos flasks from the kitchen. I can hardly believe my eyes. Thermos flasks! That's how she could keep the tea she'd made in advance hot. Here's one example where plastic has actually been a good thing. Progress indeed. Firewood is hard to come by and now when they've got a fire burning they can make tea for the whole day without wasting more wood.

While I'm talking to Lketinga, James carries on a conversation with Albert, Klaus and our bemused drivers. Lketinga's older brother is crouched down by the wall next to him, listening to this unaccustomed torrent of English. I ask Lketinga to translate for me that I would like to see Saguna again to give her my present in person. Papa Saguna says his daughter is out with the cows every day but tomorrow he'll go back and take her place so she can come here the day after.

I'm looking forward to seeing the little girl from the old days who shared a *manyatta* with Mama and me once again. At first she had been scared of my white face, but later she had pined after me when I was away fetching stores for our shop and only started eating properly again when I came back. Whenever I went down to the river to fetch water or wash clothes I used to take her along sometimes, and she would splash in the puddles and squeal with delight. Once I brought her a brown doll from Switzerland that nearly caused a riot in the village because they thought it was a dead baby. I can hardly wait to see how Saguna has turned out and whether or not she remembers me.

I sip the hot sweet tea and gradually all my stress ebbs away. The taste of the tea makes me feel as if I'm back home. Klaus finds it disgusting and Albert prefers water from a bottle fetched from the car, but to me it's like the best champagne. For days on end this sweet drink used to be the only nourishment we had.

Two little girls are sitting outside the door and I ask Lketinga about Napirai's half-sister. He turns round and says something to the two children. One of them comes into the room shyly and I immediately recognize a certain resemblance to my daughter, particularly around the eyes and forehead. Lketinga says something to her sharply and the girl makes a bit of an effort and says hello to me, but without looking up. Napirai was – and still is – shy too. I wonder if it's in her genes. Shankayon has the proud nose of her father while Napirai quite clearly has the rounder nose of her African grandmother.

Lketinga tells me his daughter goes to school, but with an almost dismissive wave of the hand. As far as he's concerned school has got nothing to do with real life, so I'm rather surprised that he allows his only daughter here in Africa the opportunity. Even though under the new government school is theoretically compulsory, it's still up to the father whether or not his children attend. Shankayon is pretty and tall for her age. Little Saruni is hopping around by her side staring at us all curiously and without the slightest inhibition.

Her father James tells us proudly that apart from the oldest brother, the whole family lives here in the corral. Even Mama moved over from the other side of the village where we used to live, to be closer to everyone else. There are no *manyattas* at all left on the hill now, everyone's moved into the village. I'm surprised and ask why. James smiles and tells me: 'You've seen how Barsaloi's grown. We now have a standpipe in the village with running water. Nobody needs to go all the way down to the river to fetch water anymore.'

Once again I'm amazed at how much things have changed in the past fourteen years. James points at a little tin shack in the yard outside: 'That is our bath and toilet,' he declares proudly. Later I discover that the toilet is a simple squat affair and the bath a bare room with a red plastic basin on the ground. But despite how simple this 'wet room' is I'm delighted not to have to go and conceal myself in the bush and then burn the used toilet paper afterwards. Between the toilet cabin and a thorn tree there's washing hanging on a line. The whole corral has a sense of peace and domesticity about it. James has really organized everything rather well.

Lketinga disturbs my thoughts to ask: 'Do you know how many shops there are here now?' I shake my head and stare at him in anticipation. 'There are fourteen shops, three butchers and a beer bar in Barsaloi today. How about that!' That really is a surprise. Sixteen years ago I was the first person to get a proper shop up and running here. When we were sold out there was nothing to be had in the whole of Barsaloi and the surrounding area. I'm really pleased to hear that nowadays there's always enough food. Everything I've seen and heard in the short time we've been here has created the impression that, although life is still rough and ready, things have got a lot easier. Certainly the financial help we've provided over the years has made things easier for my African family than for others.

As if Lketinga was reading my mind he looks at me and says: 'Really, life has got much better here. Perhaps you'll decide to stay again?' And he laughs with a flash of his white teeth. I answer rather embarrassedly but with a hint of mischief: 'You've got yourself a new young wife. Where is she then?' Suddenly he looks serious, flings his arm out at random and snaps: 'I don't know – somewhere!' Clearly he doesn't want to talk about her so I change the subject.

Every now and then James's twelve-year-old son appears in the door. He's called Albert after my publisher. The fact that they have the same names, however, doesn't seem to impress him much as every time a white face looks at him he starts whining or runs off. His sister Saruni, on the other hand, is much more trusting. Bit by bit she plucks up the courage to come over to me. She's so cute that I'd like to pick her up straight away. She reminds me of Saguna.

Stefania – in the meantime we've learned James's wife's name – is standing in the doorway to the little room that serves as their kitchen. She only speaks when spoken to. All there is in the 'kitchen' is a fireplace, although not on the ground as normal but raised so she can cook standing up. The fireplace is made of concrete with a little work surface around it and a few pots and pans and plates hanging from the walls. On the ground is a four-gallon water canister.

James asks if we're hungry, but Lketinga protests: 'No, later you must eat a goat. I will slaughter the biggest and best for you.' Albert says there's no need and, as a former vegetarian and animal-lover, makes a face. But James adds his voice: 'Absolutely, no question. What would people say if we didn't slaughter the best goat for your return!' The sight of the rather embarrassed faces of Klaus and Albert makes Lketinga burst out laughing. There are another few hours still before the herds return for the evening. We should use the time to sort out sleeping arrangements before darkness falls.

Our Camp

We walk over to the nearby Mission. Every few steps I have to shake hands as people call out: '*Mama Napirai! Supa! Serian a ge?*' The welcome after all these years is really incredible. At the gate to the Mission I recognize the doorman and another employee. We'd already been told Father Giuliani was no longer here, but a young Colombian priest welcomes us. He has no objection to us erecting our tents up here for a couple of nights. He's been in charge of the Mission for a couple of years and has already heard the White Masai story.

Our cars are brought up into the Mission enclosure and a relatively flat piece of land found to park them on as there's going to be a tent on the roof of each. The drivers set to it and half an hour later the sleeping quarters for my companions are all ready.

While the drivers are setting up a tent on the ground for me, Lketinga wanders up and stares at the roof tents in amazement. 'What is this?' he asks irritably. I laugh and explain to him that these are 'houses' for Albert and Klaus. As ever when something new and unusual is explained to him, he shakes his head and mumbles, 'Crazy, really crazy! How can anyone sleep up there?' Cautiously he climbs up a couple of steps on one of the two ladders and sticks his head in the tent. Before long we hear his amused laughter as he tells us: 'Yes, oh yes, that looks just great!'

He's almost certainly never seen a tent before, let alone one erected on the roof of a car. I know the whole business must seem extremely odd to him. It's not at all normal among the Samburu for guests to bring their own accommodation with them. Whenever they are out and about they can always rely on a roof over their head. The only thing that matters is following the rules of hospitality. I recall that my ex-husband was only allowed to spend the night in the homes of women who had a son of around the same age as him. Obviously a rule designed to avoid hanky-panky.

After Lketinga has finished inspecting the roof tents he asks with some concern where I'm going to be sleeping, here or in Mama's *manyatta*. I point to the drivers who're already putting up my tent. 'Okay, no problem,' he says calmly and goes over to help them.

I watch him in amazement. Normally among the Samburu building houses is something done by women. They cut down the thick and thin branches that make up the framework of the *manyatta*, drag them to the site and collect the cow dung and clay used to plaster the walls and the roof. As a result, houses – including all the domestic equipment – belong exclusively to the women. Men never own houses.

As youths they learn in their warrior years the art of surviving in the bush without a *manyatta*. After circumcision they leave their mother's home and live in a male commune out in the bush. During this time they spend most nights in the open along with their cattle. If it rains they spread a cow skin over their heads and wait until the sun shines and they can dry out their kangas. They are, however, allowed to keep a few personal belongings in their mother's hut and eventually spend the odd night there. But they must never eat anything in front of their own mother. Women who have been 'circumcised' – that is, married women – are not allowed even to see a warrior's food.

Yesterday evening in Maralal Lodge James was telling us how hard the warrior period was for him. He had been brought up more in the school than in a *manyatta* and slept with his fellow pupils in ordinary rooms. But then after he was circumcised at sixteen he was obliged to go off into the bush for several months herding cows and carrying out all the traditional rituals, which was something he was not at all used to. The first time he settled down for the night on a cow skin in the open air, he could hardly sleep because of all the strange noises. Every time he woke up he kept groping around him in the dark for the walls.

Meanwhile my igloo tent has been finished and Lketinga is hammering the last peg into the ground. I'm moved by how helpful he's being. In the old days when there was some work he wasn't familiar with to be done, he used to say: 'Oh, I don't know how to do that, do it yourself.' We start sorting our luggage out and I drag my two huge bags into my tent. Before long Lketinga is sticking his head in and pointing to the bags asking, 'Have you got any presents for me in there? Did James write to tell you what I'd like?' All this with a face like a small child on Christmas morning.

I have to laugh and tell him proudly that one of the bags contains nothing but presents for the family, but he'll have to wait as I'm going to give out the presents at my leisure in the morning when there aren't so many nosy onlookers around. He finds this hard to cope with and in the end just before it gets dark I give in and between us we carry the heavy bag down to the corral where James is already waiting for us.

In The Corral

By now some sixty mostly white goats have come back to the corral and everyone's very busy. The tiny kid goats are crying for their mothers and they themselves run around bleating if they're not milked soon enough. Everywhere women and young girls are milking goats. They hold one hind leg of the goat between their knees and a calabash or tin cup under the udder while they milk it, usually with the goat's own kid suckling one of the other teats.

This is the best time of day in the corral, the liveliest, when all the animals and the people who've been looking after them come home. Half an hour before the goats are due, Mama always sits outside the *manyatta* waiting for them, usually with one or two other women. As soon as she's got the first fresh milk, she starts making *chai* for the child who's been out with the goats and then cooks *ugali* for the other children and herself – the same meal every night.

Klaus is filming everything that's going on. When the children realize what he's doing they stop being so wary and start acting up for him, grabbing the baby goats and carrying them around. Even three-year-old Saruni jumps behind one of the littlest ones and expertly throws an arm around all four legs, lifting the little animal up and holding it towards Klaus with a look of triumph. He hardly knows where to point his camera next. Then when he starts showing them snatches of what he's taken on his little monitor and they see pictures of themselves for the first time they all pile out of the house and cluster around him. Before long he's surrounded by both young and old clamouring for a look at the little screen. Curiosity is the greatest ice-breaker.

While I'm sitting there watching all this revelry Lketinga's younger sister comes up and greets me effusively. She was out with some of the goats and has only just come back. Of course, she asks about Napirai and I have to tell her everything. I was always very fond of her. She was married to a much older man when she was just a young girl and he died after her first child was born. Since then she has lived on her own, though she has had a few more children, but still cannot marry again. She always had a great sense of fun and still has, repeatedly hugging me and rubbing her head against my throat.

Lketinga comes over and interrupts his sister's effusive outpourings to grab my arm and pull me to one side. In a serious voice he says, 'Come and see which goat I am going to slaughter for you!' Papa Saguna and James are already going through the herd and pulling one goat or another to one side. Lketinga joins in and the three of us white people are left standing there like witnesses to a death sentence. Eventually they make their decision: it is to be the biggest male.

Lketinga takes the animal by the horns and leads it out of the herd. At first it goes along quietly, but then suddenly starts bleating loudly. The noise is bloodcurdling. The other goats stand there chewing the cud while the big male struggles to get free. Albert goes off, saying he'll come back when it's all over.

Lketinga grabs my arm with his free hand in passing and says: 'Come and watch. It's your goat!' I know it's an honour for a woman to attend and don't show my feelings as I watch the killing ritual. Papa Saguna grabs the animal by all four legs and throws it onto the ground on its side. Immediately Lketinga puts his hand around its nose and mouth to cut off its air supply. The animal writhes and jerks in its attempts to free itself, its stomach heaving up and down. It seems to me to take forever. Thank God it's already dark and the only light is from the moon. It is a Samburu tradition that no blood should be spilled before the animal is dead.

While they're suffocating the animal silently, life all around goes on as normal. A few children are running after kids while others are watching the slaughter. At last the goat stops struggling and Papa Saguna calls on Shankayon to fetch a sharp knife and a bowl. He whets the knife on a stone and then with a practised hand slits the animal's throat. Immediately the blood gushes forth and the bowl underneath fills slowly with the warm liquid while the goat's head is tipped backwards. The animal's yellow eyes stare lifelessly at the heavens.

Lketinga asks teasingly if I want to drink some of the blood. I say thanks but no, so he offers some to Klaus who's already seen more than enough.

James takes the bowl away and in the darkness I can just make out two warriors going with him. I ask Lketinga why he's not going to drink any of the blood and he replies, 'Because I'm not a warrior anymore.' He then throws the dead animal onto a sheet of corrugated iron while his older brother slices through the pelt along the stomach from the breast to the genitals with a single cut. The little girls help him, one holding a torch, the others a leg each.

Now he begins to skin the animal, but for that he hardly needs a knife. With one hand he pulls at the pelt while keeping the body down with the other. Quickly and easily the pelt comes away from the flesh. I watch in fascination as the whole scene unfolds without a drop of blood being spilled. It takes barely twenty minutes before the animal is lying in front of us completely skinned. Now the belly has to be opened up and the intestine and internal organs removed. Papa Saguna sorts everything out neatly, laying the various body parts separately on the corrugated iron. I get out of the way as I remember from the old days how awful the stench is. After all I'm intending to eat some of this meat later.

I join the others in the house to drink hot *chai* poured from the thermos. Little Albert runs off to hide behind his mother again and watches me with fearful eyes. James starts telling us how the locals in the village reacted when I wasn't among the first of our party to arrive. 'You know, most of them didn't believe that you would really come back after fourteen years. And when only Klaus got out of the first car they thought they had been proved right. Here's a *mzungu*, they thought, come to tell us Corinne's not coming after all. But I calmed them down and told you were just visiting the school first. Then I heard people saying to one another: she's coming like a queen with two cars and two drivers. First just one car turns up and a white man gets out to explain things and set up a camera. And then she only turns up later. They all agreed: only a queen is moving in this way.'

We all burst out laughing. I really hadn't been expecting to be compared to a queen, although I was aware that turning up with two big four-wheel drives and chauffeurs was going to cause a bit of a fuss. After all, they only knew me driving my clapped-out old Land Rover myself. James repeats the story a couple of times, getting the same laughs each time. This afternoon he'd heard that even people who didn't know me but had simply heard of me were excited by our visit.

44

On my first trip to Kenya, 1986

Lketinga in full warrior dress, 1987

Lovebirds

My Samburu white wedding

A proud father and his daughter

With our daughter in Barsaloi

Nyahuru, our staging post on the way to Samburu Country

With a friend on arrival in Maralal

Meeting with James at Maralal Lodge

Barsaloi's new school

With Lketinga again after fourteen years

Revisiting old haunts

Lketinga in the corral

Getting to know each other again

Barsaloi seen from afar

The old watering hole

At long last, the meeting with Mama I had so looked forward to

Heart to heart

Flicking through photos of Napirai

With Shankayon and Saguna

Talking over old times in James's house

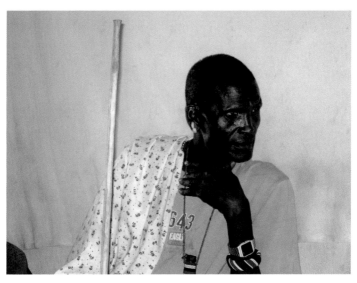

Lketinga listens to his daughter on tape

The Mission in Barsaloi

Lketinga and I chatting with Klaus the cameraman

Papa Saguna skins the goat for our welcome meal

Going back over the 'good old days'

Playing with the goats

With Shankayon, Lketinga's daughter

In Mama's *manyatta*

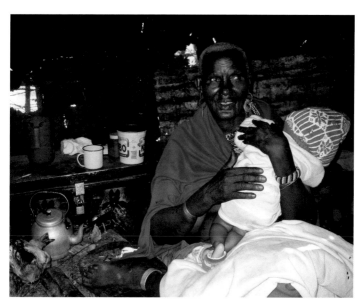

Mama nursing Felista, James and Stefania's youngest child

In Mama's *manyatta*, just like in the old days

Where our *manyatta* used to be

Outside, under the full moon and thousands of stars, there is nothing to be seen of the goat's body. Instead Lketinga is already sitting by the fire turning a few pieces of meat on a grill. It has already been decided which pieces will be served to the older men, which to the women, and which may be given to the uncircumcised boys and girls. I remember Mama cooking the offal, feet and head in the *manyatta*. I sit down next to Lketinga by the fire and watch the fat dripping from the roasting meat. It's hard to believe that just an hour ago this was a live animal standing in front of us.

We try to start a conversation but it's not easy to find the right things to talk about. When I go to talk about the book he says: 'Later. Not now.' When I try to tell him some of the things that happened after I left, he says: 'I don't want to talk about our time in Mombasa, or else I'll go crazy again. I have changed my lifestyle. I don't drink anymore. I'm content. I have three wives and I'm happy.' Well, up to a point – I don't think he's still entitled to count me among his wives but this isn't the moment to go into that. So I tell him about Napirai, our daughter, what she's doing in school, which subjects she likes and which she doesn't, that she might like to get a job instead of staying on at school. That's something he understands straight away of course: 'Yes, she is clever like me.'

They're cooking meat in the *manyattas* too now and everywhere there's the smell of smoke. Gradually I realize I'm really hungry and look forward to biting into a big chunk of meat, even if it is likely to be tough. At last everything's ready. We sit down around the table in James's house and a big metal pot filled with chunks of meat is placed in the middle. Everybody tucks in, some chewing on ribs, other sinking their teeth into hunks of leg meat. To me it's all wonderful, but Albert and Klaus only eat the minimum required by politeness.

After our orgy of goat meat we slowly make our way to our beds, tired and exhausted by the journey and all the events of the day. Lketinga walks up to the Mission with us and we agree to meet up here in the morning for tea.

Albert, Klaus and I sit down on our camp stools outside for a few moments to talk over everything we've seen and done. The drivers remind us we have a full fridge in the car and it doesn't take much for us to decide on a gin and tonic to round off the day. We're only a few minutes' walk from the village but already it seems like a different world again. I'm sitting comfortably on a camping stool with a cold drink in my hand speaking German with two white people. Suddenly the whole thing seems surreal. I've never looked at Barsaloi from this perspective before.

Klaus drags me from my reverie by recounting his meeting with Lketinga before we arrived in the village. As soon as he climbed out of the car he spotted Lketinga under the thorn tree. James was standing next to him talking to him, but then disappeared into his house. Klaus felt a bit out of his depth and didn't quite know what to do. Then he plucked up courage, shouldered his camera and went up to Lketinga. As he tried to introduce himself, Lketinga looked at him blankly for a second then turned away and continued staring down the road towards the river. Klaus felt like he was being completely ignored. After what seemed like an eternity he heard Lketinga say in reproachful tones: 'You are late!' Relieved finally to get a few words out of him, he started trying to explain why we had taken so long, but was immediately, rudely interrupted: 'I know everything,' said with an extremely disparaging expression. This got him really worried thinking, oh God, what's going to happen when Corinne gets here? How are we going to get along here for several days if he acts like this all the time? The minutes drag by, and then eventually he hears Lketinga say: 'Do you have a cigarette?'

'You've no idea how glad I was to hear him say that. Under the circumstances I was just really pleased to be able to do something he'd appreciate. He took the cigarette and said 'Let's go in the shadow.' So there we stood, the pair of us, in the shade of the thorn tree. I can tell you I've never been so glad to see anyone arrive as I was when you two turned up!' says Klaus, leaving us in stitches of laughter. Actually I really could feel sorry for Klaus, being able to picture so well his description of my ex-husband's behaviour and the sort of dirty look he can give.

But that apart, we're all agreed that the way people welcomed us, including Lketinga, has been far better than we had even hoped. I drain my drink happily as the two men climb on top of their vehicles and into their tents. I crawl into my own little igloo tent and get myself comfortable in my sleeping bag. The drivers are still sitting outside, chatting quietly to one another. From the village comes the occasional bleating of the goats and once a dog barks briefly. I can just make out human voices like a low distant murmuring. I would give anything to know what Lketinga and Mama and all the others are thinking about us and our first day together again. As far as I'm concerned I couldn't be more pleased at how it's gone and I feel all warm inside. I just wonder if they feel the same.

In Mama's *Manyatta*

The next morning I wake up early and crawl out of the tent, still fairly tired, to see the red ball of the sun slowly peeking up from behind the mountains. There's not a sound to be heard in our little camp. I wash myself with moist freshen-up tissues and settle down to enjoy the sunrise. Before long my two companions are up too and we're just having our breakfast cup of tea when Lketinga arrives. Unlike yesterday he's wearing European-style clothes, long trousers, a T-shirt and slip-on shoes. He shakes hands with us all, asks us how we slept and then walks over to my tent. As if it's the most natural thing in the world for him to do, he unzips the front of my tent and takes a good look around to check out how things look after the night. Before, when I was his wife, such signs of jealousy really annoyed me, now I can hardly keep myself from laughing out loud in astonishment.

After he's seated himself down next to us we discuss what to do with the day. He tells us James has to go down to his school on the motorbike because there's an inspection visit from Nairobi today. His older brother is still here but is intending to head home shortly before it gets too hot. I want to make sure he gets his presents before he leaves. Later in the morning we can go down to the river and then take a look around the village.

Lketinga is happy with that plan so eventually we get up and stroll down to Mama's *manyatta* where Papa Saguna is sitting outside in the shade. He says 'hello' and then announces in Maa that he wants to set off straight away so he can send Saguna to see us tomorrow. I run over to James's house to where my bag with the presents is and fetch out a checked Samburu blanket and an orange fleece top. Papa Saguna seems absolutely and genuinely delighted at these simple gifts. He thanks me with the words: '*Ke subat, ke supati pi* —

48

wonderful, simply wonderful'. We're bound to see him again before we leave as there's going to be a party in our honour. We can make arrangements through his daughter Saguna. After saying our goodbyes he sets off out of the corral, his green hat on his head and his new blanket wrapped around his hips.

Just like in the old days I use the traditional word, '*Godie?*' to ask Mama's permission to enter her *manyatta*. If she agrees, she replies, '*Karibu.*' Mama asks me in and for the first time in fourteen years I crouch down to enter a *manyatta* again. I tiptoe past the hearth to sit down on the cowhide behind it. I'm too worked up to pay attention to what I'm doing and suddenly I notice I'm bleeding from a scratch on my upper arm where I've scraped it against one of the dozens of willow branches sticking out of the walls.

Mama has got *chai* on the boil on the fire. She's holding James's little baby in her arms, nursing him gently and singing softly to him. All I can see of the baby is a little pair of naked legs sticking out of a dress; her head is covered with a big hat to conceal her face. I recall the old tradition that for the first few weeks nobody outside immediate family members is supposed to look on the face of a newborn child. The Samburu believe in a form of witchcraft and fear someone might put an evil spell on a newborn that could cause bad luck or even death. When I came home from the hospital with our daughter Napirai I was so proud I wanted to show her off to everybody but Mama insisted I kept the child indoors or whenever I took her out at least covered with face with a cloth. It nearly broke my heart.

Mama gets one of the young girls in the corral to take the baby to its mother. Despite the smoky atmosphere I immediately feel at home again in the *manyatta* and gladly accept a cup of *chai*. Lketinga sits down beside me while Albert and Klaus, after saying hello, sit down outside. Mama sits opposite on her own cowhide. This is her own special corner and no one else is allowed to be there except for very small children. Behind her one part of the wall has a sheet of corrugated iron against it covered with a blanket with a gathered-up sooty mosquito net over it. Next to her is her private lockable metal chest, the key to which hangs permanently around her neck. This is where she keeps all the most important things from her long life. It also contains a pair of mugs for tea and various cardboard boxes. Next to the hearth are a teapot and a sooty black pan. Between the hearth and her naked foot lies the severed, blood-encrusted head of the goat slaughtered yesterday. At some stage in the day she'll put that on to boil for stock. A very young kid is tethered to a small divider, dozing quietly. Next to me there is another metal chest on which I recognize several bit and bobs belonging to Lketinga, which leads me to believe that at the moment he must be living here while his new wife is building a *manyatta* somewhere. Samburu custom does not allow him to bring a third wife into the *manyatta* built by the second. I had been hoping to spend a night in Mama's *manyatta* but under these circumstances I reckon it wouldn't be a good idea. After all, I don't want to cause any unnecessary complications.

While I sip at my hot tea I do my best to follow the conversation between Lketinga and his mother, which is getting more and more animated. I ask what the matter is and he tells me there's no more cornmeal and so she can't cook *ugali* for the children, and also that some of the other women have been getting at her because we haven't distributed any presents in the form of food. He's been explaining to her that James carried everything into his house yesterday and we'll open the presents when he comes back this evening. That seems to calm her down and she's happy again. Seeing as it's a long time to wait until evening when you're hungry we go and fetch one of the sacks of cornmeal. Mama says thank you as usual but with a rather grumpy expression that is only explained when a load of other women start queuing up at the door of her hut. We go out to make room for them, and in any case we want to go down to the river.

At The River

I want to try to find the place where our old *manyatta* stood. We plough our way through the thorny savannah vegetation to the opposite side of the village. As ever Klaus has his video camera, and Albert a stills camera. When we reach the higher ground I can find only a few thorny stumps marking the site of the old corral. But there's nothing else to be seen except the familiar sandy, red-brown earth. Only the thorn tree under which Mama and the children used to sit still stands there forlorn.

Lketinga and I tell our two companions about our life here as we walk down the same track that I used for years to get to the river to fetch drinking water or to wash myself and my clothes. In the old days I used to keep meeting other women along the way but nowadays, with the standpipe in the village, nobody comes this way anymore.

As a matter of course Lketinga takes my rucksack and slings it across his shoulders. We lead the way and he asks me: 'You remember this way?' I tell him I remember it as if it were yesterday and we walk on together in silence. Every now and then my skirt catches on a thorn. I make a point of only wearing skirts here in Barsaloi as trousers on women are considered 'improper'.

We've almost reached the river when Lketinga begins to ask me about the book and the film. Somewhat reproachfully he says: 'Why is there somebody playing me, and why isn't it me? What's the point of that? Do you know this man? What has he got to do with us?' Lost in my memories of the old days, I'm completely flustered by this at first. I try to explain to him carefully that the people in the film have nothing to do with us. 'Even I'm not playing myself. It's another woman you don't even know. Mama isn't Mama and James

51

isn't James. That's the way things are in films. A lot of people in Europe have enjoyed our story and want to see what it's like here. The film will show them without them having to come here.'

He listens carefully, thinks for a minute and then says: 'But people keep coming here and telling me you were unfaithful to me, that you have your own airplane in Switzerland, lots of houses and big cars.' At first these absurd stories leave me speechless, but then I come around and ask him who these people were who've been telling such lies. 'I don't know who they are,' he says, 'but they come from all over the place, from Switzerland too, and maybe they know you. I don't know if it's all true or not. Sometimes warriors who've been down on the coast come back home and tell tall tales too.'

I feel quite upset and sad but try to keep calm as I tell him as forcefully as I can: 'I don't know who these people are! But you've known me for eighteen years. I used to live in Barsaloi and did everything I could to survive and have a happy life here with you. I would have died if I'd stayed any longer. And ever since I left I've sent money to your family despite the fact I left this country with nothing. Do you think that's normal? Do you think if I were some sort of bad person I'd have bothered with you and your family for all these years? In my country it's not normal for a wife to support her husband if she leaves him. I even sent money to you when I didn't have a job and after the success of my book, a lot more. The publishing house and the film producers have helped you too. Do you think if you were in my place you'd have done all that for me?'

He looks at me and in a quieter voice says, 'No, I don't think so, but I don't know. And I don't know why people keep telling me stories like that. Some journalists came and wanted me to tell them nasty stories about you. I told them that you're still my wife even if you live in Switzerland, that you help us and I don't see why I should tell nasty stories. I said you still belonged to our family and you're still the mother of my child. I simply refused to talk to them anymore.'

I tell him that's the best thing to do and try to explain that a lot of it's to do with envy. I remind him about the way people ganged up against us in Mombasa, about the way so-called friends spun rumours because I was young and pretty and, in African terms, rich.

'And today you get all the help you need, you have a big herd of animals, James has his own house and the film people will see to it that you have a wooden house too. If you look after the money, you need never go hungry. And all of that simply because you once had the courage to marry a white woman. I think that's the way people look at it, that possibly it makes people envious and a lot of outsiders want to spoil the good relationship we have, by making up nasty things. It's true that I have a car in Switzerland – I had a car even here in Africa. I don't own a house, like you say people told you, I pay rent every month for one. And the story about an airplane is just laughable.'

Despite how unhappy all this mischief-making by other people has made me, I can hardly suppress a smile at the thought of jetting around the place in my own airplane. Lketinga on the other hand looks a bit embarrassed now and in his gruff voice says: 'It's okay, now I believe you, really. Now you explain it all to me, I believe you. But sometimes I just don't know what's true anymore. Even James tells me all sorts of things and I just have to believe him, even if sometimes I have my doubts. I think that because he went to school he wants to make a career for himself, to become like a government minister. But I'm a Samburu, a proper Samburu, I have my animals and my family. This is okay for me.'

I take my ex-husband's hand and look him in the eyes, telling him: 'I wouldn't have come back here if I had ever done anything wrong on purpose. When I left, all I was thinking about was saving my life. And I think you can trust your brother. Who else can you trust, if not your own family?' When I've finished I have to turn my head away to conceal my emotions, especially as Albert and Klaus have almost caught up with us.

In the meantime we've reached the dried-up river bed and I'm thankful that there's a lot going on. Immediately in front of us there's a low singing sound coming from a waterhole around which a few camels are standing. Two arms appear out of the waterhole throwing buckets of water in a regular rhythm into a hollow lined with plastic sheeting. As soon as it lands the precious liquid is slurped up by the camels. As we come closer the animals turn away and gradually move off. The warrior to whom the arms belong looks up, stops singing and climbs out of the ditch. He looks suspiciously at us, replies to Lketinga's greeting and trots off after his camels. This is the time of day when from all around girls, boys or warriors bring their herds down to the river. Before long the whole river bed is swarming with goats and a few sheep of different colours. Some two hundred yards away we spot the traces of a small stream. All around the line it makes are large patches of dark sand indicating that water is still flowing just beneath the surface. Our 'washing place', where Lketinga and I used to wash each other, was a bit farther downstream from here but there's no water flowing there now.

We wander over to the herds of goats. The girls in their traditional costumes use their little sticks to try to keep their herds together. A few warriors strut among the herds. I notice that instead of the usual spears some men are carrying rifles. Lketinga explains why: 'Ever since the bloody conflict with the Turkana many people now have guns.' This new way of carrying arms makes the atmosphere almost threatening. I notice too that none of the girls are wearing the leather loincloth decorated with glass beads and that instead they all have a European-style, usually chequered skirt. On the other hand they still go bare-breasted wearing only their traditional necklaces.

There are goats bleating and lowing all over the place. Lketinga exchanges a couple of words here and there with the goatherds, and we stroll up to an unusual enormous tree that hangs over the river bed offering an inviting place to sit and rest. Lketinga and I sit on a giant tree root and from this slightly raised vantage point watch all the good-natured commotion. Klaus is thrilled to get such wonderful footage of the local colour.

Lketinga points to one young girl just coming down to the river with her herd. He recognized her from afar as Natasha. The name immediately rings a bell with me. Sixteen years ago I gave that name to the daughter of one of Lketinga's half-brothers. We were visiting him in Sitedi, and I was handed the naked newborn to hold. When I asked what her name was the mother laughed and said to me: 'You give her a *mzungu* name.' Off the top of my head I came up with Natasha. I'm pleased to see she's kept it.

And now here she is standing in front of us. I want to say hello to her so Lketinga comes with me. Of course she doesn't know me, except that I'm the one who gave the girl her name. She is very shy and won't say a word. I'm cross with myself for having nothing to give her, not even a few sweets.

When I mention to Lketinga that I wish I had something to give her, he suggests a few Kenyan shillings and then she can run into the village quickly and buy herself a nice new kanga. Somewhat doubtfully I ask who'll look after her goats for her. Lketinga has a few words with one of the warriors who has also brought his animals down to drink, and he agrees to watch Natasha's herd for her. She takes the money and runs off with great strides towards Barsaloi.

While she's away I keep my eyes on her herd too. I hope none of the animals go astray or it would turn out to have been a bad deal for the girl. Just like in the old days I find myself wondering how they can tell their goats apart. Most of them are white and to my unpractised eye all look much the same.

Back in the shadow of the tree I enjoy the panorama of the river bed. A little further on two warriors are sitting naked in the sand washing their gracious dark bodies while their red kangas hang drying in the hot sun on a piece of rock. No one pays them any attention. It is a peaceful, almost biblical scene.

A little later Lketinga says: 'Natasha is coming back.' And indeed here she is, jumping and bounding along the road with a bright yellow shawl across her shoulders. It's wonderful to see the joy she gets from letting it flap behind her. She says 'thank you' shyly and even gives me some change, which I find really touching. This present cost me so little, almost nothing really, and yet this girl can hardly believe her luck at getting a new piece of clothing. I find her happiness contagious as I watch her bounding back down to her herd like that.

For a moment my thoughts turn to Napirai, who is about the same age. It's a lot more complicated finding something for her to wear. The whole experience of bumping into Natasha has cheered me up and lifted my mood after the difficult conversation with Lketinga earlier. Even so, there's still a perceptible coolness between us.

As the heat continues to rise, the river bed gradually clears as people drift away. Then all of a sudden an old woman appears in front of me holding out her shin, the skin of which is dried and flaky so that it looks almost grey. She lets me know that she needs ointment, but I have to tell her I can't help. But at least Klaus has his sunscreen with him and that satisfies her and she vanishes as suddenly as she appeared. It's time for us to head back too. Everywhere you look there are goats lying in the shade of the trees. It's incredibly hot now and the ground is too hot to touch without shoes.

Our Old Shop

It's quiet back in the village. Everyone has retreated into their huts or found shade somewhere else, but I'm off to find our old shop. All of a sudden I find myself standing outside a dilapidated building which bears only the slightest resemblance to the magnificent big shop we used to keep. Paint is flaking off the walls all over the place, the windows have iron bars across them and the door is closed. Above it the word 'Hotel' has been scratched on the wall. I try to get a glimpse inside and then, totally unexpectedly, the door opens, almost falling off its hinges. The owner is the man who threw himself at me when we arrived the day before. It's obvious from the smell, as well as from looking at him, that he has a drink problem. He asks us in and tells Albert and Klaus at great length how hard I used to work in the shop. He appears to know the whole story of my life in Barsaloi and be a great admirer of mine, but I can't remember him at all.

When I mention it later to Lketinga, he says: 'Oh, that old boy's crazy, don't pay any attention to him.' He doesn't strike me, however, as either crazy or stupid. Some time back he took over the rental of the shop and turned it into a hotel. But then when I look around inside I get a shock: all the shelves are either falling apart or already broken. The so-called hotel is the room at the back, where we used to live, with a few hanging sheets separating it into different areas to give a minimum of privacy. But there are no beds and not even any mattresses. The man tells me his guests don't need things like that as they sleep on the floor in any case. I feel rather depressed and disgusted as I leave what was once the first proper food shop in Barsaloi and where I nearly worked myself into an early grave.

As I wander around the village people keep calling out 'Mama Napirai' in greeting, but in general things are pretty quiet at this time of day, even in my

African family's corral. The grown-ups have all hidden themselves away indoors and the children are either at school or out with the animals. Only Stefania is still around going about her business calmly and quietly with her little children Albert and Saruni. Lketinga asks me considerately if I'm hungry, which I have to admit I am now. I suggest Stefania and I cook something. The men agree and take themselves off: Lketinga, I assume, back to his latest wife while Albert and Klaus head back to our camp for a bit of a rest.

Just Us Girls

We decide to make a stew of meat, carrots, cabbage and rice. A foreleg of the goat slaughtered yesterday is still hanging from a nail near the window in the little kitchen. Stefania takes it down and hands it to me. Then she takes a huge bush knife and cuts little pieces off it, each time coming within a hairsbreadth of my fingers. I try not to think about the fact that they have no fridge and this raw meat has been hanging out in the heat. We boil everything up together in a huge pot and to my amazement, Stefania throws in a dash of ready-prepared seasoning. In my day here all they had was salt.

I try to hold a conversation with her but it's not easy, even though she has good English. She answers my question but offers nothing further. Young women here simply aren't used to having conversations with strangers or even local men.

When I take James to task about this later, he confirms, 'It's true, Samburu women don't talk a lot usually. Educated women like Stefania are better. She and I chat about things. But my brother and everyone else of the older generation believe that when you talk to your wife you should use as few words as possible and speak in good, clear sentences. They think a girl or woman who talks too much or too loudly will not make a good wife and won't obey you. It's almost always men who solve problems and make the decisions. The women simply have to get on with it without further discussion.'

Once again I realize that in their eyes I must have been very far from a perfect wife. Most of the time I was the one who dealt with problems and often after obstreperous arguments.

Despite what James says, I've never seen him chatting with his wife for any length of time or inviting her to join a conversation. She's always standing to one side with the children, listening silently or making tea. Even though she eats alongside us, there always seems to be a certain distance between us.

While our meal is simmering on the hearth, Lketinga's sister comes in and asks me to pop over to Mama's hut. I go across to find Mama dozing on her cowhide. She gets up straight away and laughs. Lketinga's sister blows on the hot ashes and immediately the *manyatta* fills briefly with smoke as the fire rekindles. She puts a pot with a few pieces of roast meat on the fire and indicates these are for me.

Mama has cooked my favourite bush meal. She's remembered that what I like most is this little dish of fried meat she makes. I'm really pleased and tuck in, although I feel guilty for a moment about Albert and Klaus whose stomachs must be rumbling by now. Mama watches me and keeps saying: '*Tamada, tamada* – take more, take more'. She smiles when I compliment her on her cooking, even though she doesn't understand the words I use.

I'm irritated by the fact that after fourteen years I can't have a proper conversation without the help of other people. How on earth did I manage back then? Lketinga's sister speaks a little and so I can make out a bit of what she says but still can't reply properly. Somehow, however, I understand that among other things she's asking for money. I pull out a couple of notes and hand the smaller one to the sister and the larger to Mama. The younger woman immediately sticks the note behind the rows of necklaces she's wearing; Mama pushes hers beneath the cowhide with her foot. Even though it's worth no more than the equivalent of ten euros, I feel certain neither of them have ever seen such large denomination banknotes. Where would Mama get money like that from anyhow? James provides her with everything they need They both say thank you with a polite '*Asche oleng*'.

James's New Life

A little while later I hear the sound of James's motorbike. I go back across to the house as dinner will be ready soon and say hello to James, who looks tired out. Saruni, his daughter, is a real daddy's girl and springs into his arms immediately. James immediately starts talking about the inspectors who've been to visit his school today, which was the reason he had to be there bright and early, even though he's feeling tired and sick. He suspects he might be having a mild attack of malaria, and there are indeed little beads of sweat on his face.

Everybody here gets malaria attacks from time to time. For sturdy, healthy folk it feels a bit like flu, and usually lasts no more than a few days. Even so it's no laughing matter: malaria is still one of the major causes of death in Kenya. Thank heavens the symptoms James is exhibiting are mild and might not even be malaria at all.

During the course of the evening I come to realize that James has almost as much day-to-day stress as the average European. He has a lot of work to do as a headmaster, runs several programmes jointly with the Mission, acts as head of the household for his family, as well as helping Lketinga build his own house, and organizes supplies for his shop. It's as if he's forever rushing between one appointment and another while the rest of the world stands still around him. It would all be impossible if he didn't have his motorbike. But because he does have it, everyone expects him to be able to do more and more. The bike has its advantages but also its disadvantages. As far as he's concerned, it's obvious that progress has automatically made his life all the more hectic.

It's not a case of getting everything done faster in order to have more free time, but of getting everything done faster in order to do even more. From a material point of view, life here has become much more comfortable for him, but his health is clearly suffering to the extent that some days he has to take something to cure his headaches before he can go to work. Very European! Undoubtedly he could do a bit less, but he's already quite clearly infected with the virus of 'success at all costs'. He says he still has a lot to learn and has registered for a further education course at the university in Nairobi.

When Lketinga arrives we all sit down at the table and a full plate of stew is placed in front of each of us. James has the appetite of two men, which makes me all the more certain that he's not really suffering from malaria. Stefania and the children spend all their time making sure everything gets served properly, while James does his best to reassure us that they'll eat later on their own. It is the tradition here that the men eat first and the women and children later. Somehow I've come to be considered a man.

Little Presents

I can hardly wait for the meal to be over so we can finally hand out our presents. At last the time comes and even Mama comes over to James's house. It's the first time I've ever seen her sit on a chair. She sits there, resting her arms on a long, thin stick, looking very dignified. Nonetheless, you can see she's not quite comfortable in these surroundings, even though she's only a stone's throw from her *manyatta*. Lketinga's sister, a brother I've never met before and a whole bevy of children have also turned up. I start with the clothing: T-shirts and jumpers for the baby, little Albert, Saruni and Napirai's half-sister Shankayon. I also have two pretty skirts for her. Next are a few more skirts for Mama, the first made from a heavy, dark-green material. Mama shows no interest. The second is a little lighter, but it's only when I produce the really bright multicoloured flowery one that she finally breaks into beams of delight. She also really likes the pretty royal blue shawl. Success at last.

The brother I don't know gets a blanket, the sister and James's wife get a skirt and a kanga each. Lketinga is watching closely and asks with a laugh if there's going to be anything for him in the bag, which by now is almost empty. I delve into it and hand him a yellowy-red blanket with which he seems well pleased, and a skirt for his wife. I didn't know of course, that he now has two wives, but as neither of them is here, it's up to him which of them he gives it to. I have shirts for all the men, a red one naturally for Lketinga. There are also a couple of cheap watches, one each for my ex-husband and his wife as well as James and Stefania. And that's it; the bag is empty.

Albert, however, has also brought presents on his own behalf for the family. Everybody takes in every detail, sitting around like children under the Christmas tree. When my publisher produces a pair of binoculars each for

Lketinga and James, neither has any idea what to do with them at first, so Albert takes both of them outside to demonstrate. James holds the binoculars up to his eyes and adjusts the focussing, then suddenly calls out in excitement: 'I can see a *manyatta* over there on the hills and two goats lying outside it, as clearly as if they were next door. Unbelievable!' Lketinga takes his time working with his too until he gets them into focus. Then the two of them stand there, binoculars to their eyes, talking excitedly to one another in Maa, of which we of course don't understand a word. It's such a comical scene, however, that we all burst out laughing, even the usually so quiet Stefania, not to mention the children. These are undoubtedly the best presents they've had today.

When everyone's calmed down and we're all back in the house again I finally produce a cassette recorder to play back the tape of my Swiss family for them. Immediately it goes quiet in the room as everyone listens to the words spoken by my mother, her husband Hans-Peter and my brother and sister. When my brother's loud voice comes on everybody laughs. Lketinga recognizes his voice straight away, nods and says in his growly voice: 'Yes, I remember Jelly and Eric. Really, I remember.' Then after a brief pause he's listening to his daughter speak for the first time. He sits there tense, his back ramrod straight on his chair listening intently without an expression on his face. When Swiss barrel organ music comes on at the end, he looks over to me and says: 'Okay, it's okay! I remember all and I wait for my child.'

James is thrilled and thanks me warmly for the recorder, although he notes that it needs eight batteries and these are expensive in Kenya. As an afterthought he adds that it's even better than the one in school. I have to explain the CD-tray to him, though, as he's never seen one before. Mama goes back to her *manyatta*, but everyone else is busy comparing presents. The two pairs of binoculars are compared, and all the material fingered and felt.

Unfortunately there are still a few children hanging around for whom I haven't brought any clothing items, simply because I didn't know they lived here in the corral and were even partly fed by James. They do chores around the house and get board and lodging in return so that they can attend the school. It seems parents who live a long way away send their children to stay with relatives in the village so as to have a chance of going to school. It breaks my heart that I've got nothing to give them other than a few sweets. We have so much stuff lying around the house at home, things Napirai has grown out of. These children here would have been delighted with any of them, even if they were too large or too small. Lketinga tells me not to worry: there is no problem about these children.

The animals will be back in a couple of hours. Before then I want to get back to our camp to have a wash while it's still daylight and warm. Lketinga sends one of the little girls into a nearby *manyatta* to fetch a plastic basin. I noticed the same sort of thing earlier when we were drinking *chai* in Mama's hut. Obviously she didn't have six cups so she sent a little girl off to borrow some from the neighbours.

It's precisely for little chores like this that grandmothers always have one of the little girls living with them. Traditionally the eldest girl of her own children is brought up by her grandmother. Shankayon helps Mama a lot when she is home from school. She has been living with her grandmother for a few months now, since her own mother went away. Lketinga has no idea when or even if his wife will be back. She's still sickly after so many miscarriages. But I notice that Lketinga doesn't pay as much attention to his daughter as James does with his. I recall him being a lot more attentive with Napirai, his first daughter, even though she was just a toddler then. Fathers don't normally have much to do with babies. Even James didn't bother to pick up or even say hello to his most recent child, in contrast to the way he treats Little Albert and Saruni.

The girl sent to fetch the basin soon comes back with it, and Lketinga rinses it out with water before giving it to me. Once again I'm touched by how attentive he is to me. I say thank you and set off back to the camp.

Everything back there is quiet and so I fill the basin with water and look for somewhere I can wash myself without being seen. A few minutes later I feel like a new woman, clean and in fresh clothes. I'm just about to set off back down to the corral when I hear someone calling me from the Mission. It's one of the employees I used to know. While we're chatting she mentions my washing problems and says: 'Corinne, you shouldn't be washing out here in the open. It's not right for a woman. Next time come into the Mission and you can use the shower.'

I take up the unexpected offer with pleasure and ask if there's any way of getting in touch with Father Giuliani as we'd like to go an see him in a couple of days' time. She says it's possible to get hold of him by radio twice a day, either at 7.00am in the morning or 6.00pm in the evening. She says we can drop by any time to use the radio. Cheered up further by this, I go back down to the others in the corral.

In the meantime Klaus and his cameras have become the centre of attention in the corral. Everyone really enjoys seeing themselves on his monitor. Many of them have never even looked into a mirror before. So Klaus spends a lot of time sitting on the ground in his light-coloured trousers with the monitor surrounded by at least eight bobbing heads. A couple of days later Lketinga asks mischievously why Klaus always wears the same grubby trousers while he changes his clothes every day in our honour.

Life In The Corral

I go across to Mama's *manyatta*. She's sitting outside with a few other women around her. Once again everybody shakes me by the hand, and I see nothing but smiling faces.

Away to one side is a woman with a baby who keeps looking over at me. She can hardly be very old, although there are already a lot of wrinkles on her forehead and big bags beneath her eyes. Whenever I look back at her she immediately looks away and doesn't say a word, but she seems strangely familiar to me. It's quite a while before I realize with some embarrassment that it's the girl whose 'circumcision' I was present for.

My God, how old and resigned to her fate she looks. To think she was just twelve years old when I peered into the 'circumcision hut' to see her sitting, smiling bravely on the cowhide, despite the fact that barely two hours earlier with no anaesthetic she had had her clitoris removed with a razor blade. She impressed me with the aura of bravery she exuded, acting as if despite her youth she was oblivious to the pain. I had crawled out of the hut ashamed that I had expected to find her a whimpering vestige of humanity. But now I have to ask myself what has happened since to this proud, happy girl.

If nothing else, she seems to have suffered from malnutrition. I say a few words to her, asking if she didn't used to be the girl who lived next door to us. She just smiles and looks away, but I persist, telling her I know she can understand my English because she went to school for a while. For just a second I'm rewarded with a beaming smile, perhaps because someone's taking an interest in her again at last.

Then her brother turns up. He's done up as a warrior but seems older and more careworn than the others of his age. He says hello to me by name. His mouth is fixed in a rictus smile that's almost spooky. Things have obviously gone really badly for their family, but I don't know what I can do to help. I can't stand in the middle of the village square handing out money: I'd only start a riot that would end up forcing us to run for our lives for fear of being overwhelmed. And I can hardly pass them something discreetly either because there are always other people around me.

While these thoughts are going through my mind I hear the first tinkling of bells and bleating of goats. Almost immediately the kids in the hut behind me start bleating too and before long you can hardly hear yourself think. The corral fills up quickly with white goats running all over the place. Mama fends off one that seems determined to get into her *manyatta*, clearly the mother of the little kid tethered inside. Then the girls and women turn up to start the milking. A few of the girls can be no more than ten years old and are carrying their little brothers or sister on their backs.

Lketinga strides proudly through the herd, adorned in his new red-and-yellow blanket, stopping now and again to examine a goat's ear or hoof. Even James has changed to welcome the goats home and is now wearing a kanga. We three white folk stand there watching all the goings-on and noticing how much more lively everything is when the children are around.

This is the time of day when people – usually elderly men – drop in to visit, usually to drink tea together. Today the man from the 'Hotel' is with them and furtively begs a few shillings off Albert for a beer. At the same time he points out a young girl of about seventeen to me and tells me conspiratorially that she is Lketinga's latest wife.

She is sitting just a few feet from us milking a goat. It would appear she has been out with part of the herd, which is why I haven't seen her until now. Considering that their wedding – and therefore the grim 'circumcision' – only took place a month ago, it can hardly be easy work for her.

I try to observe her without drawing attention to myself. She's a well-built young girl wearing traditional Samburu jewellery but comes across as rather shy and unsure of herself. It's no wonder, as she hasn't been here long and her home is several hours away on foot. She has no idea when she'll see her parents or friends again. She obviously feels an outsider here still and, apart from anything else, is living with someone she hardly knows who must seem an old man to her. The more I try to imagine myself in her place, the more sympathetic I feel towards her. As it's getting dark I can't see her face properly but I make a point of looking out for her tomorrow. It's strange that Lketinga hasn't even introduced me to his new wife yet!

James asks if we'd like something more to eat. His wife could make spaghetti. I have to laugh because back in the old days they turned up their noses at food like that even in Mombasa, saying we white people were worm-eaters. And yet now even out here in the bush they're cooking pasta. How things change! But we're all still full from the filling stew and don't feel like anything else. I make do with a cup of *chai* and the freshly produced goat milk.

By now it's dark and in the huts people are talking and cooking. First of all they make *chai* and then the maize porridge they call *ugali*. Children of all ages are running between the *manyattas* doing little chores. James is feeling rundown and feverish again and we too slowly begin to notice how exhausted we are. There are people all around us all the time and there's never a minute when you can retreat and be on your own for half an hour to chill out. All the time there are men, women and now children clustered around us talking to us in Maa, which we don't understand, or just standing and gawping at us.

I've already had several young men come to see me. Two of them were schoolmates of James and used to come by our house regularly to play cards. I'm pleased to see them and that they're doing well. However, they all have the same problem: no jobs. That's partly why they want to go into further education but they can't find anyone to sponsor them. They ask me if I can offer them any financial support but it's hard to promise something to one and not the other, and how am I expected to make a decision like that? Apart from anything else, they're all about James's age – just over thirty. I promise to think about it and make a mental note to ask some questions up at the Mission.

An Evening In The Mission

To give everyone a bit of a break we decline a communal evening meal tonight and decide to retire to our camp. We agree to meet up in the morning for a long chat with James, Lketinga and Mama. There are so many things I still want to know about the past few years.

Back at the camp we settle down on our folding chairs and our drivers Francis and John light lamps to provide us with a little light. We spoil ourselves with a drop of red wine to round off the day. As a selection of nibbles are magically produced from inside the vehicles it occurs to me that this time, as opposed to my previous incarnation in Barsaloi, I'm not going to lose any weight.

I tell the others it should be possible to get in touch with Father Giuliani over the Mission radio and we decide to have a go the next day. As we are due to be on the *White Masai* film set in two days' time we could go and visit Giuliani afterwards and then come back to Barsaloi for an end-of-trip party. It also makes sense for us to leave the family in peace for a while. We've caused a lot of disruption to their everyday lives. Even James has had to tell us that he does have to go to his school from time to time.

As we're talking over all this, four women in nun's habits walk by heading for the Mission. Then shortly afterwards the new Colombian priest appears and sits down to join us. He asks us how we're doing and how we've enjoyed our stay so far. He's very interested in how Lketinga behaved towards me and is pleased to hear that we've had no problems. He explains that James and he have worked together on several projects. For example, James is the agent and financial manager for a group of women who make traditional jewellery that is sold as far away as Nairobi. The women are paid per piece and several of them have already had good wooden houses built on the proceeds. I'm impressed to hear all this, particularly that he has been helping the women.

The priest tells us he's been here in Barsaloi for five years and arrived just after the bloody conflict with the Turkana. He also tells us about events at the Mission since my hasty departure. Immediately after Father Giuliani left in 1991 more missionaries arrived, one of whom died of tropical malaria. He was taken to Nairobi where they tried for over a year to save his life. The story sends a shiver down my spine, reminding me of my own horrific experiences of malaria. More than once I nearly died of it. The most dramatic time was two months before Napirai's birth when Father Giuliani saved me from the worst only by summoning the Flying Doctors who flew me to the hospital in Wamba literally at the last moment. It comes back to me how close a brush with death I really had.

In response to our curiosity about the Turkana business, the priest tells us as much as he knows:

'Nobody was expecting it, even though there had been a few attacks on individuals over several months and even a couple of deaths. But the occasional minor incident between the two neighbouring tribes of Turkana and Samburu were not exactly unusual. But what happened at the beginning of December 1996 took everyone by surprise. The day began normally enough. The warriors and children set off from the village with their herds as usual. But a rumour spread like bushfire that during the night gangs of robbers had been seen lighting campfires by the side of the roads. Nobody knew anything for sure, however. Then around midday suddenly some six hundred armed Turkana attacked the outskirts of Barsaloi. They swept down out of the mountains and surrounded both people and animals, driving them down towards the river bed. Anyone who tried to defend themselves, warriors with spears or even women and children, were simply shot. When people here in the village heard the first shots they had no idea what was happening. Then the first of those who had escaped arrived and told them. After a brief discussion it was decided that everyone should flee as quickly as possible, but there was only one direction they could go. The Samburu could do nothing but watch as their entire livestock herds were driven away: some twenty thousand goats and a few thousand cattle. With their own survival at stake, the people simply fled. At the time nobody could explain why the Turkana had suddenly got hold of such superior weapons. The raid was carried out like an organized crime.

'The four priests who were here at the time refused to leave the Mission and offered people sanctuary in the church. But even they were attacked, and the daughter of one of the Mission employees was killed. One of the priests had a bullet shot through his leg, and another was wounded in the arm. When the dead girl was found it was a complete shock to everyone. The Mission was evacuated at short notice and emergency aid requested from Nairobi. But it took days before anything happened. In the meantime all the Samburu warriors had got together and decided to go and get their animals back even without firearms, which they managed in large part. But it was only days later after many, many dead that the government sent in reinforcements. When one of the reconnaissance helicopters was shot down, killing a District Officer, things got serious and a few hand grenades were dropped. But by then the villages had all been abandoned and everyone had fled to Maralal.'

We asked the priest what had led up to such a massacre. 'Nobody really knows for sure. A few months previously mining companies had carried out test bores in Samburu country and found traces of gold. I'm not sure if there's any connection. On the other hand a few months earlier there had been a major incident between Samburu and Somalis in which people on both sides had died, albeit a long way away, somewhere near Wamba. But nobody can be absolutely certain what sparked it all off.'

Listening to the missionary, I remember the letters from James in which he wrote that they were all forced to live with strangers outside Maralal and had lost nearly everything they owned. Mama, thank heavens, had been got out of Barsaloi in a car just in time. Amidst all that horror she had been forced to get into a car for the first time in her life. All of a sudden they had become refugees in their own country. Many people had starved.

I helped them as much as I could but at that time I was unemployed back home in Switzerland. Two years later they were still waiting to return home. By then, however, my book was already becoming successful. The following year, in July 1999, Albert went to visit them and was also able to help out. When I think back to the photos of the family then just the memory makes me feel sick. At least today there's no trace anymore of the devastation and most of the families seem to have come to terms with what happened to them. The only thing that worries me, however, is how many warriors now carry guns.

The priest interrupts my train of thought to take his leave and turn in for the night. The three of us retire too, each mulling over the experiences of the day.

Lketinga's New Wife

The next morning I wake shortly after 6.00am. I hear a few voices from the village and decide to go over to see Mama. At this time of day it's still cool and I pull on a jumper. When I get to the corral, however, I can't get in because the thorn fencing is still across the opening. I peer over the fence until Lketinga spots me. With his new blanket pulled up over his head he strolls slowly through the herd to the 'gate', which he opens with a smile and asks me what I'm doing up and about so early. I tell him that nobody's up yet at our camp and I prefer to be down here with the animals. Also I want to ask James for a couple of eggs, as we've nothing for breakfast. James hears us talking and comes out of his house. He says hello and then gives me the last four eggs they have at present.

I turn to head back to the camp, but Lketinga sends me to Mama's *manyatta* for *chai*. I ask if I can come in and Mama is amazed too to see me up and about so early. Two elderly men have just been in for *chai* and are leaving the *manyatta*. She hands me a cup and at the same time puts the pan of roasted meat on the fire. I'm amazed that there's any left. Obviously she'd made it just for me and won't give any to anyone else. She presses a soup spoon into my hand and encourages me with her usual, '*Tamada, tamada,*' and then goes out. Delighted and embarrassed at the same time, I eat a few spoonfuls of the meat for breakfast. I'm almost certainly the only one to be offered such a luxurious meal so early in the day.

I'm chewing the meat, lost in thought, when suddenly Lketinga's young wife crawls into the *manyatta*. She obviously thought it was empty, given that Mama and Lketinga are standing outside with the animals.

Taken aback, she stops in the entrance, still bent over but uncertain whether to come in or go back out. I smile at her and say, '*Karibu!*' She comes in and, cautiously avoiding Mama's place, sits on the cowhide near the fire. I move along to make room for her, waiting to see what she's up to. She opens Lketinga's metal box and takes out the skirt that I brought for his wife – whichever one he wants to give it to! She feels the material carefully and then checks out the size before immediately placing it back neatly. With my minimal knowledge of Maa, I ask her if she likes it. She gives a shy 'yes'. Then she turns around and is about to leave the hut when Lketinga comes in. It's his turn to be surprised but doesn't say a word to either me or his young wife, who shrinks away and crawls out of the tent.

I have to suppress a smile when I see how serious Lketinga looks. He sits down on a little stool in front of the entrance near the fire, takes a soup spoon and fills it with meat. I use my spoon playfully to push the pieces of meat back into the pot, protesting: 'No, that's my meal. Mama made it specially for me.' He smiles back, acting the beggar: 'Only a little bit.'

Of course I give him some, but I can't resist mentioning his wife and, as if in passing, say to him: 'That was your new wife, wasn't it?' He looks serious and says: 'Yes, do you have a problem with that?' I say no, of course not, but ask him: 'Why don't you speak to her or at least look at her?' 'Why should I say *Jambo* to my wife first just because I'm her husband? She's never said hello to me, so why should I say hello to her? It's up to her to speak first, then maybe I'll speak to her.'

He says this with such conviction that, despite the awful tragedy of the situation, I have to laugh out loud. Obviously unsure of himself, my ex-husband begins to laugh too and says that's normal. I try to tell him things could go on like that for months and it would be better for both of them if they gradually started talking to each other. He admits he doesn't know her very well, but he's spoken to her parents and asked around the village about her. He knows a lot about his wife's background. I discover she comes from the little village near Maralal where I was first struck by all the plastic bags hanging on the bushes. I realize that means she will only see her former home rarely or perhaps even never again. I ask him how he expects their marriage to be tolerable if they don't talk or laugh together. 'Yes,' he replies, 'that's crazy! But I'm not going to talk to her first, I'm not a woman.' Then he adds with a laugh: 'Maybe I should marry you again.' I join him in a rather nervous laugh of my own, which, under these bizarre circumstances, seems the safest thing to do.

Then all of a sudden I realize I've left the eggs sitting on James's motorbike and with a twinge of guilt remember my hungry travelling companions. We leave the hut and stroll up to the Mission. They're already making tea and coffee, and Albert, Klaus and the two drivers are pleased to see the eggs. Apart from some nuts and a few soft potato crisps, that's all they have for breakfast. They're surprised that I'm not hungry but I tell them how spoilt I was in Mama's *manyatta*.

After the frugal breakfast we go back down to the corral with Lketinga. We bump into James who's busy spraying the little *manyatta* where the kid goats are kept with pesticide. That's something they didn't have in the old days either. While we're chatting, Lketinga's sister comes out of Mama's *manyatta* and greets us effusively. But Lketinga speaks to her gruffly and rather sharply, and she runs off. I ask him what's wrong and with angry gestures he replies, 'Last night my sister was drunk. I don't allow that and don't know how it could have happened.' I immediately remember the money I gave her and Mama and feel somewhat guilty.

Heart To Heart In The *Manyatta*

In the meantime James has washed his hands, and now he and I crawl into Mama's *manyatta* and sit down on the cowhide. He's going to translate so it's best if he sits next to me. Klaus follows and sits himself down on the little stool next to the hearth. Lketinga sits down near the entrance, whereas Albert contents himself with saying hello but staying outside in the shade. He can hear everything just as well from out there; a *manyatta*'s walls may protect against prying eyes but they are far from soundproof.

As ever Mama is cradling James's baby as she welcomes us. Today she's wearing one of the new skirts. James starts by telling her I've a few questions for her. She looks at me and nods her agreement. The first thing I want to know is what she felt when James told her I was planning to visit. '*Ke supati pi* – wonderful,' she says, 'I was very pleased, but I couldn't believe it anymore than anyone else could. Nobody here in the village thought you'd come back after such a long time. But next time bring Napirai, my little Napirai.'

I have to laugh at this because by now my daughter is already taller than I am. But for Mama she remains a little girl, like she was the last time she saw her. Then she adds that it's been good for everyone to see me again after such a long time. Lketinga nods in agreement and says: 'Really, this is very good! But nobody believed it. Even when the first car arrived, all the women said: 'There's something not right here, Mama Napirai's not coming after all, we knew it.' Then James repeats what some of them said: 'Only a Queen is moving in this way!' and all of us, including Mama, break into laughter.

Klaus asks what she thought way back the first time I came to Barsaloi and she saw me here. Mama's face grows serious as she thinks for a moment and then says: 'I was just afraid.' I ask her what she was afraid of, and James does his best to translate: 'Because a white woman was something I'd never come across before. I wondered how I was supposed to talk to her if she didn't understand me. She was bound to be used to a very different way of life and yet here she was coming to live with us in a smoky hut. We had almost nothing to eat and survived mainly by drinking milk mixed with blood. There were so many thoughts filling my head that I was simply terrified. I was also thinking what use is this white woman going to be to me? All my sons' wives are like children to me. Their problems are my problems and vice versa. But in your case I was worried there would be even more problems. You wouldn't be able to fetch firewood, water or food for me because you were a white woman. Who was going to wash my clothes and do chores for me – not this *mzungu*! It would all be the other way round: we'd have to do everything for you. At first I could see nothing but problems. On the other hand, Lketinga had told me you'd come all the way from Mombasa to see him. So I had to give you a chance, and you stayed. And you worked hard. You looked after me and fetched water and firewood better than any of the others before you. You brought me food whenever you could and everything worked well, and so I came to love you.'

I'm listening to this with tears running down my cheeks. I had no idea how much worry I'd caused her back then. She continues, telling us that the village people had all come to her hut wanting to know what sort of *mzungu* I was. Why did she let me sleep in her hut when she didn't know me? How we could have any sort of conversation when we couldn't speak to each other? 'In time I replied to all of them: 'I get on with her well and she does her work. She doesn't cause any problems and doesn't start any arguments.' After a few months I couldn't see any difference between you and the other children, our own ones. You became my child. From that moment on I became responsible for you and your problems became my problems.'

Through all of this I'm having to wipe away tears and am deeply embarrassed at the same time because I know I shouldn't cry. Mama looks at James and asks him what's the matter with me. Quickly I ask him to explain to her that this is a *mzungu* way of expressing strong emotions and feelings and she shouldn't worry or think there's anything wrong. James translates and suddenly she's smiling again.

Lketinga finishes Mama's account for her: 'Yes, it was very difficult at the start. The other warriors came to me too and asked why I'd brought a white woman back. I was the first warrior to bring a *mzungu* woman to Barsaloi and marry her. Everybody came out and looked at us suspiciously, and some of them said bad things about white people. Even the little local government boss-man came and asked why I hadn't requested his permission to marry you. I am a man and he expects me to ask another man who I'm allowed to marry. Crazy!' And we all break into laughter again.

Now it's my turn, and I tell them that when we were living in a village in Switzerland shortly after we arrived all the other children ran away from Napirai because she was the first mixed race child in the village and they weren't used to seeing a baby with a dark-coloured skin. But now there are lots of dark-skinned people even in the smallest villages and over time people have got used to it. Mama nods and says, 'There we are then, and it's just like here!'

James tells us that over the past few years there have been more white women turning up in the area around Maralal and living with Samburus, even though they haven't gone as far as living in a *manyatta* like this one. Lketinga gets a laugh again by saying in his rough voice: 'But these are mostly old ladies and not as good as you. I wouldn't have married one of them.' James has to agree and says: 'It's true, Corinne went everywhere with you. She went with my brother to visit relatives who live in places with no water or where the cattle live inside the corral, like in Sitedi, and she had no problems.' Well, I think to myself, it's not exactly true that I had *no* problems.

Mama is still cradling the little baby and says: 'I was so happy that you gave me a grandchild, and I was proud that you trusted me with Napirai when you had to go away for a bit. That was the greatest proof of your love. After that I had no problem accepting you and couldn't see any difference between black and white. We were all the same.'

Suddenly Mama's face stiffens and becomes expressionless and I realize that what she's doing is concealing her emotions. Then she quickly brushes her free hand across her eyes. I had always felt there was a deep bond between us, but it's only now, fourteen years later, that I have the proof.

For a few seconds we all go silent, the only sound the buzzing of flies around our head, and outside the cackling of hens and bleating of a few goats.

Then we hear Albert talking to the children outside the hut; it seems he's drawing something for them in the dirt.

James turns the conversation back to the little boss-man, the 'Mini-Chief' who's a sort of village policeman: 'All he wanted from you was almost certainly money. People here think all *mzungus* have loads of money, live in big houses, have cars, lots to eat all the time and nothing to worry about. They think they all live like presidents. I keep trying to explain to them that white people have worries too but just don't tell everyone else about them. It's a Samburu tradition to spend a couple of hours talking to everybody you meet. The older person always begins by saying where he comes from, who he is, how his family and his animals are, who's sick, what's wrong with them and what's been going on in the corral or village where he lives. And then he'll finish up by saying where he's going and why. The one who's doing the talking goes into every detail and it can easily last an hour. Then it's the turn of the other one and it all starts over again.'

James acts out one of these meetings with an imaginary dialogue and has us all in tears of laughter with an act worthy of a cabaret. 'It's perfectly normal here,' he goes on, when we've all recovered from laughing, 'because sometimes people walk for hours on end and see nobody. So they're happy when they run into someone to talk to, even if it's someone they don't know. When they get to their destination, they tell people there who they met on the way and what he had to say. And so the conversations get longer and longer but in a few hours news can spread like wildfire over great distances. And then they see white people who chat to one another for only a couple of seconds before going on and think these people obviously have no problems as they've got nothing to talk about. The thing is the whites just don't talk about all their problems.'

It just goes to show how differently people see things. Our society is losing the art of talking to one another because there is increasingly little direct communication between us. It's something that's harming our society but these people here, on the contrary, see our inability to talk to one another as proof we don't have any problems.

But James is talking again: 'I almost live like a *mzungu* now. I work very hard and have so much to do that I only ever travel by motorbike. When I come across people on the road, they stop me. At first I used to think it was something important and stopped the bike. But usually they only want to know where I'm coming from and where I'm going. Or they want to look at the bike and have me tell them all about it. But I don't have the time. I just answer their questions with 'yes' or 'no'. Sometimes I don't even mention that someone at home might be sick because it would take too long. But then if they find out I haven't mentioned something like that I get it thrown back at me next time I see them. People just don't understand that I have a timetable to stick to because I have obligations. It doesn't matter to them if they stand around for an hour or not'.

From the way he talks it's obvious that he's actually proud of being one of the first out here in the bush to lead a new, modern sort of life. But I regret the way he's talking because it sounds like the beginning of the end of the natural way of communicating with one another. Eventually many people will end up lonely as is already the case in Europe. Klaus suggests that with James rushing all over the place on his motorbike he must miss out on the little things of life. James replies that times are changing fast. Lketinga doesn't agree with him though: 'I don't like it. Nowadays the *moran* [warriors] don't wear their hair long the way they used to. The girls don't wear as much jewellery because the schoolboys don't give them any. Schoolgirls like my daughter Shankayon have hardly any jewellery at all now because it's banned in school. They don't even want to rub red ochre into their skins. Even those who don't go to school prefer to use face cream from Nairobi. None of the girls wear skirts of animal skin decorated with beads the way you remember my sister did. They only put these things on for ceremonial occasions.' James adds: 'And even that'll be gone in five to ten years. Already you hardly see the traditional neck decorations made from giraffe hair or ivory earrings on warriors.'

I find all of this really depressing, although we've been partly responsible in bringing modern things here. Only now do I realize that I haven't seen a single young girl or warrior adorned with the full glory of jewellery and paint that they used to wear fourteen years ago. And yet it was precisely the joyful intense colours of their jewellery and their kangas that expressed the vitality and intensity with which these people lived. If, over time, the beautiful red and the deep blues and yellows of the cloths and blankets should fade and give way to the drab uniformity of European clothing, then the optimism and sheer joy of these people would also ebb away. More than a few of them already consume alcohol in considerable quantities. A lot of the young people now have a basic schooling but they don't have the money to go on and learn a trade or go into further education. They end up living in their own society but with western attitudes and ideas and as a result they give up on their own traditional way of life. It seems to me that they're losing their roots.

The longer we talk, the more relaxed everybody gets, and eventually I pluck up the courage to ask Lketinga how he felt when he realized I wasn't coming back. He looks at me gravely and says: 'At first I simply didn't believe it because in the past you had always come back. I soon started having problems with the shop because trade fell off and so I got into difficulties over money. Everybody tried to cheat me. When the car caught fire, I had no money to repair it. So I sold the big car and bought a smaller one. I used it as a taxi until I had an accident and was put in jail. I ended up in a whole lot of problems and I'd really rather not think about it.'

James continued for him: 'When I heard how things were – three years after you had gone back to Switzerland – I went back down to Mombasa to find him. Lketinga was in a bad way when I found him. I asked him to come home with me, which was what he wanted to do anyway. We agreed to meet up the next morning to get the bus to Maralal. But he didn't turn up, so I went back on my own as I had to be back at school the next day. But a day later, when I was still waiting in Maralal for a lift to Barsaloi, Lketinga suddenly appeared on his own, and so we came back here together. Obviously he had nowhere to live and nothing else to his name except for a lot of animals. During the years when he hadn't been here his herd of goats and cattle had grown substantially. Our older brother had looked after them for him. It's the custom here that no one would sell or slaughter someone else's animals.

'So, despite everything, Lketinga was rich when he came home. We decided that the best thing would be for him to find another wife who'd build a house for him and have children. So one month later he married his second wife, Mama Shankayon. After her first child, however, she had a lot of problems: all their other pregnancies miscarried. Now she's gone home to her parents and we don't know when she'll be back.'

Lketinga just nods absently while Mama listens in silence. I feel quite keenly that my ex-husband neither can nor will talk about his past anymore. To change the subject he starts talking about the book and the film and gets James to tell us about the way the success of my book went down in Barsaloi:

'Well, as you know,' says James, settling into his stride, 'we've had lots of strangers coming here, mostly Kenyan journalists, asking if we know what's in the book, that Corinne has written nasty things about the Samburu and got a lot of money for it. But each time we tell them that we know what the book says and we get money from it too and have no problems with it. It's our family she's written about and we're the only ones who can judge whether what she says is right or wrong, true or false. We have even been in touch with a Kenyan ambassador who speaks German – and is a Samburu – and he has reassured us that it's all okay. When they hear that, most of the journalists go away again, but there are always one or two who want us to say something bad about the book or the film. They've even offered us money. One of them even suggested to Lketinga he ought to go to the District Officer and demand that this Corinne woman be jailed in Switzerland. When he did that, Lketinga got really angry and told her to clear off and leave him alone. But she still kept pestering him.'

Here Lketinga joins in again: 'Yes, they were really crazy. I kept telling them that I'm not going to do anything of the sort, that you're my wife and it's fine by me if you're leading a good life in Switzerland. What matters to me is that my child is well looked after. I'm fine and I don't need as much as you do in Switzerland. And you have no goats or cattle. But they didn't give up until I threatened to give them a thrashing if they didn't clear off. The things they were saying were getting to people here in Barsaloi.'

'Even the priest,' adds James, 'who had read the book in Spanish spoke to people and told them there was nothing bad in it. But now everything is back to normal and everyone is really pleased that you and Albert, the publisher of the book, have come here.'

At that moment Albert himself crawls into the *manyatta* to say that he's known me for a long time and knows how much my African family matter to me and how much I worried when things weren't going well for them. He and his family have for years now felt tied up with our fate and as a result even he feels close the people of Barsaloi. He was always certain he wanted to make this journey to get to know this family and particularly their magnificent Mama. He also regarded it as an obligation to offer what help he could. James translates all this for Mama, and she thanks Albert with a handshake and the familiar words, '*Ashe oleng*'.

Finally Albert asks Mama what she expects from her future or what she would wish for. She thinks for a moment and then says: 'I'm okay actually. I hope my health will last and my eyes will still be able to see. But even if I should go blind, I'd like to think I could still lead as good a life as now, and I hope that's the way it will be. I don't need anything else.' James confirms what she's just said, telling us he offered to have a house built for her but she refused. She preferred to stay in her *manyatta* and is just happy that everyone's together now. Sometimes she won't leave the hut for up to three days on end but is happy because she always has visitors or children come to see her. It's nice to see that at least the old people remain as fully integrated into communal life as ever.

Asked if he has any special wishes, Lketinga, to my amazement, says: 'I would like you not to tell people that you are no longer my wife. We don't do things like that. It doesn't matter where you live: you are still my wife. I don't want to hear of another man living with you. It's okay, but I simply don't want to hear about it. I will always consider you to be my wife and I hope that from now on you'll come more often, because Samburu don't drift apart.'

I'm very moved by his words but at the same time I feel he's asking too much and trying to place restrictions on me. As gently as possible I try to explain to him that, after such a long separation, it's normal that I might not want to be on my own forever. After all, he's got married again, twice over! I say this with a little laugh to try to defuse the tension. He replies: 'Yes, it's okay, but let's just not talk anymore about it.' It's a good thing that I didn't mention in any of my letters to James that I'm no longer together with my partner back in Switzerland.

James says it's hard to find the right words at times like this and gets us away from such a sticky subject by telling us his own hopes for the future: 'I would like to extend my house so I have more room for visitors. My guests should have somewhere comfortable to stay. Apart from that I'd also like a mobile telephone so that from Maralal at least – where you can actually get a signal – I could communicate more quickly and easily with other people. There's no network yet in Barsaloi and won't be for some time. I would also like a television to find out what's going on in the country and the rest of the world, to find out what's happening in Germany even or Switzerland.' With a laugh he says that's the end of his wish list. 'I don't need anything more, for the moment.'

Saguna

Outside the *manyatta* we hear voices now and Lketinga says it must be Saguna. I'm pleased and curious to see her. We bring our conversation to an end after nearly three hours and crawl out of the hut. The bright sunlight blinds me. Albert sits down on the stool again and is immediately surrounded by children drawing in the dirt. A little further off I spot Lketinga's wife building a new *manyatta*. The young girl is already weaving the willow branches into the framework of the walls.

Stefania appears and tells us Saguna is waiting for us in her house. The first thing I notice on entering is Lketinga's sister sitting on the green sideboard with a serious look on her face. Saguna is hiding behind her, done up from top to toe in traditional dress and looking simply radiant. When I left the village for the last time she was just four years old. And now here she is standing in front of me as a well-built, good-looking girl of about eighteen. I tell her how delighted I am to see her. She's a bit shy but I tell her that in all these years I've never forgotten her. I had asked after her in my letters and been told she was almost a fully-grown woman and no longer living with Mama in her hut.

Saguna is wearing a red skirt with two kangas, one blue and one yellow, slung around her shoulders, covering her naked breasts. Yellow kangas are worn only by girls of marriageable age who have not yet been 'circumcised'. Around her neck and lying on her breasts are row upon row of beads. On top of these red rows of beads she's wearing an unusual, brightly coloured piece of flat jewellery almost like a plate. Taken altogether, she must be wearing some five pounds of jewellery. Around her head she has a headband of closely set beads with a little cross attached, also made of beads, with lots of little

85

metal strips hanging from it. On her forehead is a button made of mother-of-pearl with a metal cross hanging from it down to almost cover her nose. Attached to this are two fine metal chains that stretch left and right across her cheeks to link up again with the headband. Behind all of this, Saguna's features appear soft and dainty. It suddenly hits me that she looks incredibly like her late mother, who sadly died in childbirth when Saguna was barely eleven years old. Luckily at that time she was still living with Mama.

It's obvious she's not used to being the centre of attention. Girls are only the focus of things at their wedding and at the 'circumcision' that accompanies it. The birth of a girl is normally no big thing for a father. He would try not to be present at the birth. But if the newly born should turn out to be a boy, there are lots more rituals to be carried out than if it's a girl. The neighbours, therefore, soon know the sex of the new baby, even if because of fears of witchcraft they don't actually see it until weeks later.

Saguna sits there with her hands in her lap, looking at me shyly but with curiosity. I pay her compliments that she accepts with some embarrassment. Given that I know she's had to walk for four hours in the heat to get here and must be hungry and thirsty, I ask James to offer her something, but he simply says she'll get something in Mama's *manyatta*. I gather that there is some form of social taboo at work here. Saguna is a young, 'uncircumcised' woman and therefore can't be served food or drink in James's house, as he was, until recently, a warrior.

So I suggest the she goes to see Mama first and we can talk later. When she's left the house I ask James when she'll get married. He doesn't know and even Lketinga, when I ask him later, can't tell me. It strikes me that at eighteen she's on the old side for an unmarried girl. But she must have a boyfriend among the warriors or she wouldn't have so much jewellery, which counts as a sort of status symbol for girls. The more jewellery she has, the more sought-after she's considered, and her marriage price can rise as high as seven cows or more. The sad thing is that the girls are never allowed to marry their boyfriends. All he gets to do is prepare the fat and red ochre that the bride rubs into her body.

Marriages are mostly arranged by the father. He makes sure the wedding has nothing to do with looks or sexual desire. What counts is the reputation of the girl's family. The wife-to-be will have to produce children, run the household and look after her husband's animal herd until the children are old enough to take over the task. Sometimes the bride even has no idea who her husband is going to be. Those most sought-after are the ones who have just finished their time as warriors, as men are not allowed to marry earlier. If a girl is unlucky she can be married off to an older man or even some geriatric as his third or fourth wife, and then she has to do what his first wife says.

I'm upset and worried by the idea Saguna might face such a fate. I ask James if there isn't some way of preventing anything like that happening to her. 'No, Saguna only knows our traditional way of life and you can't change things. Everything has to take its course. She will go through her ceremony and then have a new home with her new husband.' He says this so matter-of-factly and with such self-confidence that I can see it's going to be a very long time before women here have any right to a life of their own.

Then all of a sudden I realize how absurd and hypocritical my attitude is: on the one hand, I'm lost in rapture at how colourful and beautiful the traditional clothing of the young girls and warriors is and wish Samburu traditions could be preserved as long as possible, while on the other, I'd like to see those customs and rituals which offend my European sensibility changed. It's a painful insight to live with and at the same time I'm glad my own daughter Napirai has grown up in Switzerland. She's about two years younger than Saguna and if she were living here, she'd have no chance of leading her own life, no matter how hard I might have fought for her right.

When we leave the house a little later I spot Saguna sitting on a stone under the thorn tree, playing with Shankayon and two other girls. I sit down next to them and wait and watch. She's taken off her pretty headdress because it's too hot, and from time to time she has to put her hands under her necklaces to lift them up and let the air at her skin. Suddenly she asks me about Napirai. I try to tell her what I can, which because of the linguistic problem isn't much. Instead I ask Shankayon to go and fetch the little red photo album from Mama. Meanwhile Lketinga has turned up to translate a bit for me.

I ask her if she remembers me, if she recalls the brown doll I brought her and the way we used to go down to the river together. She nods earnestly in response to everything. Then Shankayon comes back with the album in her hands and gives it to Saguna. She flicks through it, beginning obviously with the most recent pictures of Napirai. She stares at them in amazement and asks if it's really Napirai. Lketinga explains in details to her the pictures of Napirai in the snow, on the ice or swimming in a lake. She takes them all in with enormous interest and something akin to astonishment. It must be something extraordinary for her to see a girl just a few years younger than herself who was born in the same place but now lives in such a radically different world. For a start she must find if strange to see Napirai with long hair. Her own head is shaved because people here don't find girls or women with long hair attractive. She lets her gaze linger long on the pictures of my daughter in jeans. I would give anything to be able to read her mind right now.

By now there are lots of people gathered around looking at the album, and Shankayon more than anyone seems delighted by the pictures of her half-sister Napirai. Saguna keeps flicking through the book from front to back and giggling and whispering to the other girls. I move a little closer to her, admiring her slender arms and her rows of different coloured bangles. After a while she turns to me and asks: 'Why didn't you bring Napirai with you? Where is she now and who is she with?' I tell her that she's in school and while I'm away she's staying with the family of a girlfriend. Lketinga translates this for her and says that perhaps she'll come when she's finished school.

Saguna listens, stroking my arm gently. She's obviously fascinated by the silver bracelet I'm wearing, in which she can see her reflection. Her tender gesture brings back to me how close we were when we lived together in Mama's *manyatta*. In those days she was my little ray of sunshine who brightened up the day when I was feeling down. I feel helpless when I think of her possible fate and the fact that I can do nothing to protect her from it. On the other hand maybe she wouldn't want me to, maybe she'd prefer to be accepted and respected by her tribe. I make a wish with all my heart that she finds a good young man.

Klaus meanwhile has been taking more pictures, and it seems Shankayon has told Saguna they can see themselves on the monitor. She sits down beside Klaus now and he demonstrates the camera for her. At first she seems shocked and then amused to see the moving pictures. She's never seen herself like this and is fascinated to watch every last bit. She gets Klaus to rewind and fast-forward and her childlike wonder gradually infects us all. Unfortunately it's almost time for Saguna to set off on the long walk home. Tomorrow it's back to life as normal out in the bush, minding the herd. I give her the things I've brought for her: a pretty frock, some nice-smelling soap and a body lotion. She's delighted by her presents and packs them all up in her kanga. When we say goodbye I know I'll never see her looking so natural or so colourfully dressed again.

New Eating Habits

James has invited us to dinner in his house. Stefania hands out aluminium plates and puts a big bowl of spaghetti on the table. We all tuck in heartily, even though it's not exactly the way we normally eat it. Stefania has broken the spaghetti into little pieces and mixed in vegetables and lumps of goat meat.

James tells us that some of the villagers, especially in families where the children have been to school, have changed their eating habits. He's known spaghetti since his school days and so doesn't find the dish unusual for him or his family. His children have grown up eating it. I want to know if Mama eats pasta nowadays. In the old days she would have refused to try anything she didn't know. The only exception was pineapple. James laughs and says: 'No, Mama won't eat it but she still likes pineapples and whenever I bring one, she starts talking about you. You got her to like them.' I remember it well and can still picture her slowly and cautiously biting into a piece of pineapple.

When I ask James if the Somali shops are now selling these things too, he gets quite worked up: 'There aren't any Somalis here anymore. We got rid of them all. Do you know when you left Barsaloi and the only Samburu shop was closed, the price for maize meal and sugar soared? Instead of sticking to the official state prices, the way we did, they doubled them. Everybody in the village started complaining and bad-mouthing them. 'Why isn't Corinne here anymore?' everyone kept asking. 'Now we don't have a shop or a car.' The Somalis charged too much for the few things they had and didn't pay people as much for the goatskins and cowhides as you did. Lots of village people kept coming up to me and asking: 'What can we do to bring Corinne back? Only *mzungus* can run a shop like that, and there aren't any others who want to come and live with us like she did.' They even suggested I should offer to marry you to get you to come back! They were so worked up about it all, people were suggesting the craziest ideas.'

I sit there quietly drinking my tea as if to help me digest all this – the idea of James and me getting married is a new one on me, and I have to laugh at the idea. James shares my amusement at the idea and goes on: 'I told them we should work together to open our own Samburu shops so that we can keep a check on prices. Gradually one shop after another opened up till we reached the point where we are now, when there are too many, and business is not so good for any of them!'

At this point Lketinga comes and in and sits down on the sofa beside me asking with a long face if we've been talking about him. For some reason or other he seems to be in a worse mood than he was an hour ago. Nobody seems to know where he's been or what he's been up to. For a brief moment it occurs to me that maybe he's feeling left out, like he used to do fourteen years ago when James came home from school with his friends and we enjoyed ourselves playing cards together. In an attempt to cheer him up I ask if he can still remember the spaghetti dinner we had in Mombasa with my brother Eric and his wife Jelly. It was a mad occasion because all the locals thought we were eating white worms. In his rough voice he says, 'Of course I remember. I thought it was plain crazy. And now we even have people here in the village who eat that stuff.'

Road Maps

Later on we sit down to work out our plans for the rest of the trip and decide to drive down to the film set tomorrow as agreed, spend two days there and then go off to find Father Giuliani before coming back to Barsaloi.

That way the family can catch their breath and get back to normal a little before they have to prepare the big all-comers feast they're planning before our departure. Unfortunately as we're the guests we're not allowed to contribute much, although as the family will be doing all the work we'd like to offer to cover their expenses. They're going to slaughter four goats and cook up an enormous amount of rice and beans. But before they get that far they're going to have to collect a vast amount of firewood and make several fires for cooking, all of which involves a huge amount of work with no car and not much time. James says he'll sort out the food and asks Lketinga if he could buy a few goats, but he answers rather abruptly: 'No, I won't have time. I'm going with Corinne to see the film set. I'd like to know what they're up to!'

Oh God, I think, feeling suddenly quite ill at the thought! That's the last thing I need! I know I'm going to find it difficult enough taking in the film set and understanding the movie-making process. I've only a very vague concept of what to expect and how I'm gong to cope with it. But the very idea of having to explain it all to Lketinga again is more than I can bear! He doesn't have the first idea about what making a film involves.

I suddenly vividly recall the scene we had when Lketinga and I went to see a film in the Mission in Barsaloi – the epic *Ben-Hur*, of all things. Lketinga got incredibly worked up over the whole thing and would not believe it had nothing to do with *mzungus'* modern everyday life. He was absolutely convinced that the film represented modern life in Germany or Switzerland.

Only twenty minutes into the film we had to walk out and the rest of the evening was spent in argument while he refused to believe that the film had nothing to do with real life.

And now he wants to visit a film set where they're making a movie about the Samburu and a part of his own life to boot! How on earth is he going to understand that he's not going to see a finished film but a series of shots that are probably incomprehensible out of context? No! This is simply not something I can deal with, especially as I'm nervous about the whole thing myself.

Thanks God James finally intervenes in the discussion on our side, telling Lketinga he's going to be needed here. He can hardly be absent, after all, when the entire village is getting ready to put on a party for his guests. He sees the point of that and promises he'll wait here for us instead and deal with buying the goats.

Glancing at the clock, I realize it's time for me to be on my way to the Mission if I'm not to miss the chance of contacting Father Giuliani on the radio. When we get there the attendant welcomes us and shows us into the room where the transmitter is set up. It's an ancient box of a thing and I can hear various voices in different languages – Italian, Swahili, English. Lketinga listens closely, obviously understanding more than I do, and after a minute or two he nudges me and says gently that I should say something.

All of a sudden for the first time in more than fourteen years I hear once again the voice of Father Giuliani, just as strong as ever. He's obviously delighted to hear we're here and tries to give us instructions on how to get to him. But it all sounds so complicated that all of a sudden he says he's prepared to come and pick us up from the Mission at midday in three days' time. I'm just about to tell him how grateful we are when I realize the connection has already been lost.

We stroll back to Albert and James in the corral where the animals have once again returned and it's the usual colourful evening scene, with all the women milking the bleating goats. Lketinga's sister takes me by the arm, presses a cup in my hand and urges me with a laugh to have a go at it myself. I pick out a big fat white goat and am delighted to get a thin little spurt of milk into the cup. It seems, however, I need a bit of practice and I have to admit that even a three-year-old child here is better at milking. Before long there's a crowd of children gathered around me laughing. But it's precisely this '*joie de vivre*' that I love so much here. Despite the hard conditions they live under, people haven't lost their sense of humour. The children chase the baby goats here and there, laughing and giggling like children at play anywhere in the world. As it gets dark, people begin to brew up maize porridge and tea and we retire to our camp. James and Lketinga are due to drop by in an hour's time.

Back at the camp we collapse on the little folding chairs and the drivers John and Francis come over. They're extremely friendly and helpful, keeping watch on the cars and all our stuff during the day. As usual they offer to fix us a drink, but we decline as we'd prefer Lketinga doesn't see any alcohol when he turns up. I don't want to put any temptation in his way because up until now at least I haven't seen him touch a drop in public.

Four of the sisters from the Mission are sitting in meditation up by the water tank. Their rough-haired little dog comes down to see us, and Albert and Klaus make a fuss of him. So we all sit there quietly for a while enjoying the silence and keeping our thoughts to ourselves. This reunion that I had longed for and yet dreaded for such a long time has in the end exceeded my wildest expectations. I feel really happy and at peace with the world. On the other hand, it's perfectly clear to me that I could no longer live back here. Even if some aspects of life have got easier, things are still rough and ready at best. If nothing else, the slow repetitive pace of daily life here would eventually get on my nerves. How on earth did I manage before? The only thing I can imagine is that I was so in love with Lketinga and, at the same time, just the business of staying alive was an effort.

And now here comes Lketinga, strolling towards us slowly with his familiar elegant stride. He says he's just seen two goats he wants to buy but intends to wait until we've left as the price is likely to drop then. He's going to send word to his older brother too, to invite him to our farewell party. While he's talking James comes up and exchanges a few words with the priest before sitting down beside us. He's also busy with preparations for the big party in four days' time. We ask him with some concern if there'll be enough food for everybody. 'This isn't a problem for Samburu,' he reassures us. 'It's our tradition that everybody is invited to a party like this and nobody can be turned away. But if there's nothing left to eat or drink, then it's no problem.

We're not obliged to keep providing food until everyone has eaten their fill, and given that we fully expect half the village to turn up, there's not much chance of that in any case. The most important thing is that we have enough tobacco for the old folk.' Lketinga nods in agreement and says he's sure it'll go fine. After another half hour we say our goodnights and agree to drop by the corral in the morning before we head off. As he leaves, however, Lketinga asks me: 'You sleep good alone here, no problem?' pointing to my tent. I laugh and reply: '*Hakuna mata* – no problem, and good night'. Then I crawl into my tent and fall fast asleep.

Off To The Movies

I wake early next morning uncertain of what it is that's disturbed me. Listening to the sounds from outside I realize that, apart from the dozens of different bird calls that greet us every morning, there's the long low baying of a donkey mixed with the barking of a dog. It's still a relaxing change to feel so much a part of nature and not have wake up to the sound of traffic and car engines. I crawl out of the tent eager for what the day will bring.

Our drivers are already up and about, clearly keen to get their vehicles back on the road. Before long we're all standing around the gas cooker waiting for tea or coffee. The nuns' funny little dog, whom we've christened Willi, is already getting under Klaus's feet, which makes us all laugh. All there is to eat are the last few crumbs of potato crisps and a few nuts, which hardly appeal.

Francis and John stow away the roof tents with practised ease, and we pack up our belongings before heading down to the corral. Lketinga meets us coming up the hill, and James is already standing by his motorbike, ready for the off. We go over final details for the party and give James money to buy what's needed. Mama comes out of her hut to say goodbye, but it's not too traumatic as we all know we'll be back in a couple of days. I throw my arms around her and tell her I look forward to seeing her again shortly, and she smiles in acknowledgement. James revs up his bike and sets off, leaving a cloud of dust in his wake as always. Shortly afterwards our drivers arrive to pick us up. Lketinga avoids my eyes but touches me gently on the arm and says, 'Lesere – auf Wiedersehen!' He walks away slowly then turns round to ask, 'Are you coming back after two sleeps or three?' I tell him, 'Two. But we'll only be here for a little while to meet up with Giuliani, and then we're going on to Sererit. We'll be there for one night so after three sleeps we'll be back here for the party.'

'Okay,' he says with a serious face, 'Off you go then.'

Once more we drive down the dried-up Barsaloi river bed past the school and then shortly afterwards take a turning towards Wamba. There are never any signposts here so you have to have a good idea where you're heading, especially as all the roads through the bush look the same: red earthen tracks with only rare lane markings, frequent potholes and crossed every now and then by the beds of dried-up streams. The landscape is incredible, dotted with vast numbers of thorn trees and here and there a little bush ablaze with hug red flowers in the middle of this semi-desert, proof that nature can cope even with very little water. It is beautiful to look at. On the horizon I can see the mountain ridge with its thick jungle to which the wild animals retreat during the dry season.

For the first time the sky is no longer an unremitting blue, but dotted here and there with fleecy white clouds. In a few weeks' time the rains will come and then the whole region changes with astonishing rapidity. The rivers swell so quickly that they carry everything before them in a rage of reddish-brown waters and become impassable for days on end. The earth – now red, parched and dusty – will be transformed into a sea of mud. This is all something we'd actually rather not experience on our short safari and hope the film crew avoid it too. I let my eyes roam over the magnificent panorama and, as I look more carefully, gradually pick out individual corrals scattered here and there across the plain. They blend so well into their environment that it can be easy to miss them unless you spot the telltale circles of thorn bushes.

Even though we're not going very fast, it requires a lot of concentration on the part of our drivers. Animals scared by the noise of our engines lurch across the road. Camels in particular find it hard to get out of the way quickly as most of them have one of their forelegs tethered up at the knee and can't move very fast on just three legs. It's not nice to see but it does seem to be a useful technique for keeping the herds together.

Every now and then we come across children of all ages standing by the roadside waving or holding out empty hands. I can't stop myself giving out the last of our sweets, particularly when most of them look as if they've just got the best Christmas present of their lives. Almost all the women we come across have either a baby on their backs or a pile of wood or water container on their heads. Just occasionally there'll be a donkey to carry the load. The people stand out from a long way off with their multicoloured clothes. To our eyes, they appear majestic the way they carry themselves so elegantly across this hot, barren plain, their red, blue and yellow kangas fluttering from their bodies in the wind. The jewellery and body paint they wear make them seem all the more impressive.

Occasionally we see tic-tics, little deer-like animals, scurrying along. These are considered a delicacy in times when food is in short supply. Here and there we spot small herds of zebras. But there's no sign of any big animals, such as giraffes or elephants, although large piles of dung lying around make it obvious herds of elephants have passed by fairly recently. Between the thorn trees there are termite hills sometimes up to six feet high, fantastic abandoned insect cities. The new priest in Barsaloi told us he wants to use this material, which is as hard as rock, to build the new church in Opiroi. He says it could hardly be more suitable: incredibly hardwearing and costs nothing.

We've been on the road for nearly two hours now and it's time we were looking out for the spot where we have to turn off the road and head into the bush. Klaus has already been out to the film set twice before this trip but previously he came from a different direction. He's heard that they've laid a new access road to the set. There are indeed lots of vehicle tracks to be seen now but none of them look as if they were made by trucks. The film set is somewhere near Wamba – which I can already make out in the distance – so it can't be far.

The closer we get to the film set the more nervous and fidgety I become. Up until this moment my thoughts have been taken up primarily with my African family, but now my nerves are gradually getting the better of me. I'm particularly nervous about meeting Nina Hoss, the actress who's playing me. I really hope that we get on with one another. It can't be easy for her either, meeting the woman whose life she's supposed to be portraying. And what about the 'male lead'? Will he do a good enough job as Lketinga, even though he's neither a Samburu nor a Masai? Obviously I have my doubts.

On the other hand, it was always equally obvious that a traditional Samburu could hardly play the role. How could he play someone's life on film if he didn't even know what a film was? Or if he'd never even spoken to a white woman, let alone had physical contact with one? Traditional Samburus almost never show signs of affection, and kissing is an absolute taboo. How could a warrior possibly be expected to play this role for three months, sometimes repeating scenes as much as twenty times? It would never have been possible. The producers tried in vain to find someone among the Samburu and Masai down at the coast who are familiar with tourists but in the end opted for a pleasant but worldly-wise African, even though he's not even from East Africa. So now I can hardly wait to see whether or not I'll share the praise the directors have heaped on him. I really hope so.

It's certainly a strange feeling to be on your way to a film set where what they're filming is part of your own life. Most of the time I don't have a problem keeping the two things apart, reminding myself that this is just a film and not really my own past. But every now and then I find myself hoping that they will get it exactly as I remember it. I suspect it's not going to be easy and hope visiting the set like this will reassure me.

I'm so tied up with my own thoughts that I barely notice that we're not having any luck in finding the right way. A couple of times what we think is the right route ends up in a dead end and we have to do a U-turn. It's only by the time we almost reach the outskirts of Wamba that we come across a jeep with a big yellow sticker reading '*The White Masai*'. Klaus recognizes the people in it as members of the film crew and has them tell him the way to the set. Several miles further on we come across a signpost in the middle of the scrub with an arrow and the words '*White Masai* Location'. Seeing this turns my feelings of trepidation into something more like pride.

We twice cross the meandering but luckily dried-up bed of the mighty River Wamba before we reach the entrance to the camp. All around the area is a security fence and guards, and entrance is by permit only. Lots of men and women, most of them in traditional Samburu clothes are crowded around the gate. Some of them have set up little stands to sell items to members of the crew. We park the vehicles and for the first time in my life I'm about to walk onto a film set – and a film set of the story of my own life. I can hardly believe it!

On Set

The first thing that strikes me is that it's a genuine tent city, with proper tent houses laid out in neat rows on either side of a long central avenue, each one the exact same distance from the next. It's not hard to tell these are Germans. Every tent looks like a little house with a porch. Behind them some distance away is a row of installations covered in plastic sheeting that obviously serve as showers and toilets. My first impression is one of absolutely dumbstruck amazement at the vast amount of resources deployed to depict my life back in the days when all I had to my name was a hut made of cow dung.

The tent village is beautifully situated in the shelter of two hills with the mountains shimmering in the distance. We're taken to an information tent equipped with all the latest technology: everywhere there are people at desks working on computers and laptops, with mobile phones plugged into chargers. I'm glad that at least now I'll have the opportunity to talk to my daughter, who must be waiting with rather mixed feelings for some sign of life from her mother.

We introduce ourselves to the few people present. As it's lunchtime, most people are either eating or back on the set. Everything here is done with military precision, and we are each allocated one of the magnificent tents while they send off a messenger to inform the person in charge of looking after us that we have arrived. In the meantime we head off to the showers to wash away the dust of the road. I find my own tent and am stunned to see a proper bed with fresh bed linen and white towels: incredibly luxurious after what we've been used to the past few days. There is even a little table and chair and a wardrobe to complete the effect.

An African appears outside the tent to ask if I want hot water for my shower. Given that the outside temperature is hovering around forty degrees,

I tell him I can do without. I have him explain the shower to me, however. It's rather ingenious. You slip inside the plastic sheeting cubicle behind the tent and stand under a showerhead with a string attached which works like a toilet flush when you pull it. The water, either hot or cold depending on what you asked for, comes from a tank above, which is filled on demand. The other part of the cubicle contains a toilet, which works on the earth-closet system rather than being attached to a water flushing mechanism, but it all seems very hygienic, practical and simple.

After freshening up under the shower I'm pleased to be able to put on a pair of trousers again. I've barely got dressed, however, before someone outside the tent says, 'Madame, your lunch please.' I unzip the door and think this has to be a dream: there's a boy standing there, smiling with a tray and a silver cover over it. I sit down at my little table and can hardly believe what he uncovers: a starter, main course, dessert and various pieces of fruit, all arranged beautifully. I devour the lot with gusto. It's incredible how your attitude to eating can change when you've had to make do and give up a lot of things for a while. I remember the phenomenon all too well from the days back in Barsaloi when we were nearly starving. In those days I had money enough but no way of buying even the simplest foodstuffs because for weeks on end the rivers were impassable, and there was simply nothing available. Right now, on the other hand, I feel like I'm on a luxury safari.

After this magnificent meal I go to find Albert who's already sitting talking to the producer Günter Rohrbach. We greet one another with hearty hellos and he asks me for my first impressions. For now all I can comment on, I tell him with a laugh, is the *mzungu* bit as I haven't been on the actual set yet. He offers to show us the corral straight away and says tomorrow he'll take us to where they've built a replica of Barsaloi. It takes just a few minutes' drive for us to get to the corral they've built for filming. I'm enormously impressed. Everything is absolutely perfect; the *manyattas* look just like Mama's back in Barsaloi.

Given that the Samburu extras actually live here, obviously the way of life is absolutely authentic too. Mothers with their little babies are sitting around outside their huts, some cleaning the children, others washing kangas. There are various items of clothing laid out on the thorn stockade to dry. That is the only different I notice initially: everybody – adults and children – has clean clothes, almost certainly because they have access to the water that's brought in daily in tankers for the film crew.

Apart from that, the *manyatta* village looks as if the people have been living here for years. Everything is perfect down to the last detail. I'm really pleased to see that nothing's been bodged. Girls in pretty traditional costume pass by, but I notice that instead of bird feathers they've got plastic flowers in their hair. This looks ridiculous to me but I realize that for them plastic is something new and different and both the girls and their warriors see it has something special and luxurious.

We wander around the corral, attracting minor interest and some slight amusement from the inhabitants. None of them know that I'm the one who used to live like this among their tribe or that it's my story that's being acted out here. Before long we come to a *manyatta* that's not lived in and is slightly bigger than the others. It's explained to me that this is the one they use for internal shots and is supposed to represent the one I used to live in. Obviously I simply have to crawl inside and am delighted once again to see that everything has been recreated as accurately as possible. These first impressions reassure me that at least the film will show, and in some little way preserve, the unique culture of the Samburu, which I fear may not last much longer in its present form.

It's teatime, and once again we're presented with a luxurious assortment of juices, tea, coffee and various titbits. We've got out of the habit of having such a spread laid out in front of us but enjoy it all the more. Word has gradually got around the camp that the 'real white Masai' has turned up. Someone says to me: 'It's really nice to meet you in person. You've had an extraordinary life. I'm in awe of you. If it hadn't been for your courage back then, none of us would be here now to see this magnificent landscape and get to know the wonderful Samburu people. Thank you so much.' I'm very moved by all this but haven't a clue what I'm supposed to say in response.

I wish now that Lketinga could see this side of things for once, to understand how many people all over the world have shared our story and wish the best to him and his family. I experience all this daily back home reading all my post and emails, or in person when I do readings, or people stop me in the street. But back in Barsaloi it seems all he gets is bad news. I feel a bit sorry that he's not here to see and hear all this. I console myself with the thought that I can tell him all about it at the party and send him pictures later.

I get the chance to chat to a few of the film crew: the costume mistress, who's from South Africa originally – the whole adventure out here in the bush has made her feel homesick – and the make-up artist, who's from Germany. Someone points out the mobile phone mast that's been erected just for the duration of the film shoot. They have huge generators to provide power for everything. It's quite incredible how much stuff they've had to ship out here into the bush! I can only hope that the rains don't come early and catch them by surprise!

During the afternoon, life in the camp all but comes to a stop in the intensity of the shimmering heat but with evening it all comes to life again and people pour back from work into the tents. Paraffin lamps are set out to mark the paths and water for the showers is heated up over open fires while people busy themselves in their tents. Most of them were away all day shooting at the recreated Barsaloi. I can hardly wait to see that set tomorrow.

Albert, Klaus and I are already sitting in the dinner tent with the producer, watching them prepare food for well in excess of a hundred people. There are several Kenyan cooks working under the direction of Rolf Schmid, a German who has been living in Kenya, working in the restaurant trade for years. He is an experienced professional when it comes to providing a catering service for film crews in Kenya. Film crews who have benefited from his gastronomic expertise include those who worked on *Out of Africa* with Robert Redford and Merlyn Streep, as well as the German actress Caroline Links' film *Nowhere in Africa*. Most people in the business rate him the best caterer in the whole of Kenya. I'm hugely impressed and amazed by the sheer logistics of what he's undertaking here, especially taking into account that everything has to be brought in huge trucks all the way from Nairobi.

Little by little the tent fills up. I'm pleased to see the director Hermine Huntgeburth again. I really liked her at our first meeting and got the impression my story was in good hands with her. I'm also pleased that it is a woman directing. At last Nina arrives. Immediately it's clear to me that at least superficially she fits the bill: tall, thin and blond, just the way I looked eighteen years ago. I can even relate to the aura she gives off, which is a good sign. We say hello, full of curiosity about one another, and sit down to eat together. The situation is a little odd, however, and I feel slightly inhibited and get the impression she does too. Diagonally opposite is an Italian actor who's playing Father Giuliani. I like him even if he doesn't look much like the 'original'. At any rate I can imagine him gesticulating as energetically as Giuliani did.

Then at last I meet Jacky Ido, who is playing Lemalian, the name they have substituted in the script for Lketinga. He's dressed normally for dinner and seems to me nothing like a Samburu. I try to conceal my initial annoyance and when I say hello to him notice that at least around the eyes there is a certain resemblance to my ex-husband. When he starts talking too I find he gives off a warm, pleasant aura. He's about the right size too. I'll be interested to see what he looks like tomorrow after make-up. He tells me that it takes two hours every day to turn him into a traditional Samburu. As he has no objections, I decide to go along and watch this transformation take place.

Listening to people talk, I realize they're all really exhausted. It's a long day shooting out there in the heat. The meal makes up for a lot though, with a dessert buffet to rival any four-star hotel even though it's laid out under the stars in the bush.

Much as I enjoy luxury like this today, back then when I lived out here it would have meant nothing to me. It was my love for Lketinga that gave me such strength and will to survive. I felt it like a living thing within me that gave me the power to move mountains. Here, on the other hand, are people simply struggling to work for three months under difficult conditions. The beauty and romance of this landscape must pale for them when they're far from home and their loved ones. I can imagine what it's like and wouldn't mind asking a few questions, but I get the impression that now is not the time.

The producer makes a little speech, introducing me so everyone knows who I am. Almost immediately after dinner, however, the leading actors turn in for the night. Nina wants to go over her lines for tomorrow, and Jacky has to get up really early for his two hours in the make-up chair. So we have a last glass of wine together and head out of the dinner tent.

Off to one side there's a campfire burning with a row of chairs in a semicircle around it. I sit down and gaze into the flickering flames. After a little while a Samburu mother and a lively eight-year-old girl come to join me. The woman says hello and starts talking to me in Maa. I do my best to guess what she's saying from the few phrases I understand. Then all of a sudden it dawns on me that she's trying to explain that she knows me from way back when. She was in the hospital in Wamba at the same time as I was giving birth to my daughter. She was having her last, that is her fourteenth, child! I can hardly believe the bits of information I'm stringing together out of the avalanche of unfamiliar words pouring over me. When she goes on to tell me that she's the film-Mama, I can't cope anymore: I absolutely need an interpreter. I need to know what she's saying.

Quickly they find someone who knows both Maa and English. It seems I've got the right end of the stick. It's incredible. After auditioning dozens of Samburu women, the one who ends up playing the role of my mother-in-law is someone who knew me back then and even gave birth to a child in Wamba at the same time as me! I'm enchanted by the discovery and convinced it's fate rather than chance.

The lively little girl is playing the part of Saguna, although in the film she's called Christine. She's as bouncy as a rubber ball and in search of security, that's as plain as pie. I'm told later that she's being brought up by an aunt, either because her parents are dead, or because they've given her away. It's hard to find out anything else because the Samburu don't like to talk about the dead.

Watching this 'film-Mama' for a while, I decide I really like her. However, in comparison with my mother-in-law, she strikes me as somewhat too young and lacking the older woman's mystic aura. But sitting here around the campfire and having just heard her story I find myself bonding with her. She tells me she knows some of the members of my family from Barsaloi. I'm delighted to hear it and interested to see how she plays her role. Mama obviously was an important figure for me. She kept me from a lot of distress and gave me a lot of inner strength. If they manage to get any of that across in the film, I'll be more than pleased.

By now all the chairs around the fire have been taken and, as usual amongst Africans, everybody's nattering away. They always have some story or other to tell and most of the time the atmosphere's always jovial. The film-Mama, however, gets up to go to bed as tomorrow will be another long day on the set. I take my leave of the campfire too and after saying a few goodnights make my way to my tent.

Lemalian Alias Lketinga

Early next morning a loud dawn chorus of birdsong wakes me. I clamber out of the tent just in time to catch the sunrise. A few yards away there's a thorn tree with bird's nests, little round balls stuck to the branches with a little narrow round entrance from beneath. It's funny to watch the birds popping up into their nests from below. There must be at least three dozen of the things on this tree with their inhabitants flitting to and fro.

After making myself ready for the day I stroll over to the caravan where the make-up artist has set up shop to watch Jacky undergo his transformation into Lketinga, otherwise known as Lemalian. There's no way I want to miss this. He's already in the chair and greets me with a beaming smile.

The make-up man tells me Jacky is always good-humoured, even though he's the first into the chair in the morning and the last to leave each evening. On the wall hangs a long red wig plaited Masai-style. It looks remarkably like the real thing. I settle down to observe the transformation.

First comes the laborious task of fitting Jacky's ears with larger artificial pierced lobes to hold the ivory earrings. To my unaccustomed eyes, this soft brown thing looks absolutely macabre, like a real piece of human ear. I'm so fascinated by it that the make-up man gives me the piece they used yesterday. The first thing that comes into my head is: I must show this to Lketinga. But I soon drop that idea, realizing the sort of difficult conversation it could lead to. If I find it disturbingly realistic, how can I explain to him that there are materials that can be made to look like anything and that there are even people who do that for a living?

With extreme precision the false ear extension is fixed to the real thing and glued on behind. Imagine having to go through this same process every day. Then the heavy wig is fixed on his head. The more Jacky comes to look like a Samburu, the more I like the look of him. But as the whole process has already taken over an hour, I dash off to the breakfast table to make sure I don't miss out. When I get back half an hour later Jacky is almost finished. A traditional Samburu helps him with the body paint and makes sure that everything looks right.

Yes, I think, now this Lemalian looks a lot more like Lketinga than Jacky did last night. With his shining naked torso decorated Samburu-style, he looks magnificent and fascinating. His soft eyes and enticing smile only add to the positive aura he projects and I'm convinced now that the public will take to him. My cynicism has finally been overcome. Perhaps it's also better for me if he doesn't look exactly like Lketinga. It will make it easier for me to keep some distance between the film and the reality of my own past.

Time's getting on, however, so we have a few photos taken together before Jacky has to be driven off to shoot today's scenes, which are set in our shop. They're doing a scene in which Carola – the name given to my screen persona – is six months' pregnant. I'm interested to see how Nina will look with a 'baby bump', but also how they've reconstructed our old shop, the village of Barsaloi and the Mission building. They don't, however, want to be disturbed while shooting, and despite my curiosity I can understand that.

Barsaloi Resurrected

Before long we're on our way to the film-set village. We crest a hill and suddenly I'm struck dumb by the sight that meets my eyes. The entire village has been recreated almost perfectly. On either side of the street stand a few wooden huts with rusty tin roofs and paint peeling from the walls that makes them look as if they've been here a dozen years at least. The village sits on an area of raised ground with a magnificent view over the plain while the reconstructed Mission building stands on a slope off to one side.

As they're shooting over in the shop, we start our visit at the Mission. Even from the outside there's a certain resemblance to the one in Barsaloi, primarily because of the little vegetable garden. Father Giuliani loved his garden and had to use all his cunning and imagination to protect it from the wild animals. Here too they've planted vegetables and maize to be correct down to the last detail. The inside has been done up in colonial style and even the great fireplace dominating the room looks as if it's been used countless times. A pair of old chairs alongside an antique table, shelves full of books and paintings of saints on the walls all come together to create the harmonious impression of a room in a Mission. Outside there's the church with a superb view over the village. The producer, who's obviously enjoying showing off, tells us they'll be filming up here this afternoon.

There are people everywhere. Before they start shooting, a megaphone orders silence everywhere, even three hundred yards away from the action. That makes it virtually impossible to have any sort of sensible conversation. It's all go, outside the shop over in the village. All of a sudden someone calls to us that they've stopped for a break and we can come over to the village.

Outside the houses a few native extras are sitting on the ground and I wonder what on earth they think of us *mzungus*! One day a lorry-load of *mzungus* drives up and within a couple of weeks they've built an entire village and even a Mission building in the middle of the scrubland. Then they do everything they can to make it all look as old as possible. A bit later I watch as, for one scene, a group of native warriors and women run from one end of the street to the other, ten times over, the same thing repeated over and over again. I would give anything to know what they're thinking. One thing, however, I'm sure of: they'll be talking about this for years. Even the generations to come will almost certainly hear all sorts of versions of the story.

We're almost at the shop when we see Lemalian and Carola coming out. They both look terrific. Nina has got her hair tied back for the role, just like I used to do. With her pregnant belly, brightly coloured flowery dress and Masai jewellery she looks very like the Corinne of those days. I tell her so with absolute conviction. We have a few photos taken and then they have to get back to work. Just before they do I take the opportunity to have a look round the reconstructed shop. Yet again they've got everything just right, even the old set of scales with the stone weights. Seeing this after all these years reminds me what bone-breaking work it was lugging hundreds of pounds of cornmeal, sugar or rice every day. Sometimes my back was so bad, I could hardly move in the evenings. The best payment, however, was the smiles on the faces of my customers, just pleased they had somewhere to buy food. But my reminiscences have to give way to the work of the moment as the filming recommences.

Outside, Klaus and I go off looking for photo opportunities. I'm struck by one in particular: two very old men in traditional dress, one of them with a very unique piece of 'jewellery' – glasses with lenses half the size of his head – and a funny floppy hat with a picture of a tiger on it. I sit down for a chat with them and we have our photo taken together. The face behind the giant glasses beams at me with good-natured pride. I find the old people here fascinating for you can see their whole lives in their faces.

Then we sit down in the shade and watch the shooting from a distance for a couple of hours, but it's the same thing over and over: a few lines, then silence, then they wait a bit, then they say a few more lines, then they go silent and wait again. It's fascinating at first but soon gets monotonous if you're not up close and involved, so I'm pleased that after lunch when they're shooting up at the Mission they ask me to come onto the set.

The director offers me a seat next to the camera. I have no idea what scene they're shooting and sit there in anticipation. All of a sudden Lemalian runs up the steps of the Mission and the priest hurries over to him. It seems Lemalian is telling him that Carola and the baby in hospital are okay.

Watching this scene, I'm suddenly overwhelmed by the most appalling feeling of desolation. I had simply not anticipated this as I was feeling relaxed and comfortable with it all, but the moment Lemalian opens his mouth it's not him I see but Lketinga, and the desperate situation I was in then comes flooding back to me. I'm in such a state that I have to leave the set in tears, ashamed and embarrassed in front of the whole crew. One tiny little episode like that and I completely lose control of my emotions. What on earth will I be like when Carola comes on? There are going to be tears for sure.

Luckily it's coffee break and nobody outside notices the state I'm in. I put my sunglasses on and have a cup of hot tea. My hands are shaking so much I spill it all over one of them, but at least the pain's a distraction.

After my experience on the set close up, I decide I've seen enough of the shooting and feel I'm in any case redundant. I've seen everything, got to meet most of the actors and actresses and seen how successfully they've recreated the setting. There's nothing more I can do here to help the film along and it makes no sense for me to hang around on the set any longer. Clearly the emotional excitement of the past few days has upset my internal equilibrium. The trip to see Father Giuliani is just what I need. I always felt safe and sound in his reassuring presence. Even now seeing him is bound to restore a bit of emotional stability before I have to go back to Barsaloi to face the painful farewells with my family there.

We spend the rest of the afternoon chatting in a relaxed atmosphere with the producer and his wife. Over a splendid evening meal I thank them all for their kindness and above all for the chance of a glimpse behind the scenes of 'my' film, and tell them I have no fears and am convinced the film will appeal to a wide audience.

Father Giuliani

We set off after breakfast from the film location for the three-hour journey back to Barsaloi where we're due to meet Father Giuliani at midday. We arrive exactly on time to find Father Giuliani waiting for us. He's hardly changed. Only his white hair and a few more wrinkles in his tanned face betray the passing of the years. He is dressed – as always – in shorts, a polo shirt and beach sandals. He comes up to say hello with a broad smile on his face. Grinning he looks me up and down and says: 'What? Is this supposed to be the Corinne who was forever knocking on my door?' I have to laugh. When he knew me of course I was at my thinnest. These days I eat healthily and don't consider myself fat but I'm no longer a beanpole. He says hello to Albert and Klaus with an enthusiasm that shows how much he enjoys the break in routine that visitors bring.

Then he takes a look at our four-wheel drive vehicles and reckons we can get away with just using one. But, as our drivers refuse to let their vehicles out of their sight, that would mean leaving one of them behind and we don't want to do that. We have no idea yet how cramped things are at Giuliani's place. All he says is that his new Mission isn't as big as the one here. When I tell him that the thing I miss most of all is his pretty little garden with its banana trees, he says dryly: 'These new priests aren't interested in gardens or vegetables. They can't fix their own cars either, which is pretty essential around here. Still I suppose that's why there's a nunnery!'

I go with Giuliani in his little Mercedes Unimog truck so we can talk *en route*, but the engine noise and banging in and out of potholes means it's hard to make ourselves heard. We drive for mile after mile along the dried-up bed of the Barsaloi River towards the mountains. After half an hour's drive the scenery is already new to me. I never came so far in this direction with Lketinga. In places here the river bed is up to three hundred yards across and it's easy to imagine how dangerous it must be when the rains come.

We drive through different zones of vegetation. One minute the landscape is green with lots of bushes and so-called 'thumb palms' that I've never seen before. The next the riverbank becomes a cast dark cliff wall. Father Giuliani says there's a rumour there might be gold somewhere here and talk of test bores, which would be disastrous for the whole area.

He drives the same as always, fast and furious, a 64-year-old forever looking in his rear-view mirror and asking, 'What's happened to your young drivers with their supercars?' On the left bank of the river we come across a group of Samburu women with lots of children sitting in the shade, cooking up maize porridge in a big pot to feed the little ones. Giuliani says that around here very few of the women still have husbands who support them. Most of them have moved into the growing villages or towns and more than a few of them have taken to drink. The priest gets out to talk to the women and pats the head of a few of the children. Through European eyes, they make a pretty picture all sitting there in the shadow of the tree, but these mothers have to struggle just so they and their large brood of children can get by.

As we drive on, the bed of the river changes from loose yellow sand to dried cracked red mud. It reminds me of fragments of broken pottery distorted and fractured by the heat. I'm keen to take a few photographs of some of the shapes but the instant I step out it's like climbing into an oven. In our bare feet we couldn't even touch the earth here. Yet despite that we keep coming across people and animals who live their day-to-day lives in this hostile environment. Father Giuliani calls out to every man, woman and child we pass, his voice battling against the speed with which we're travelling. It's easy to see how well he knows and loves this part of the world.

After two hours or more we leave the river bed and turn onto a dirt track that only someone who knew it was there could have found. This takes us up hill to where a magnificent view across the great plain spreads before us. Giuliani stops and climbs out. He shows us a bush from which he plucks little balls that smell like incense and points into the distance to a little white vertical line on a far mountain that looks like a waterfall. 'That's where my

Mission is,' he says. 'A couple of months ago part of the mountain behind my house collapsed with a noise like thunder. Ever since it's been easy to point out Sererit from a distance. Next time you come you just have to head straight for it.'

We make our way towards the mountain slowly over the bumpy ground. Up on the ridge thick jungle begins and Giuliani tells us it's virtually impenetrable for human beings and there are huge herds of buffalo and elephants living in it. The Samburu bring their animal herds up to the edge of the forest because the grass there is at its most luxurious.

Completely unexpectedly we suddenly come across a long low building by the side of the road that Giuliani proudly tells us is the new school. He says the problem is keeping enough teachers; most of them simply stop turning up after a couple of months. But it's going to be a while yet before there's someone who's grown up around here and is capable of becoming a teacher. We trundle along the track making detours around the bigger rocks and bushes. Giuliani tells me the whole area used to be covered with boulders and scrub vegetation and he had to clear a track himself.

The Sererit Mission

We crawl our way up a long slow winding road until eventually we come around one last bend and find ourselves at the Mission. It doesn't exactly look like a Mission building though. My first impression is that we're in the middle of a collection of outsized tin cans. Apart from the 'church', which dominates the little settlement of no more than a few huts, everything is made of corrugated iron. Even Giuliani's trusty old motorbike is housed in a corrugated iron shelter. Our cars are almost as big as any of the dwellings. Now I understand why we should have brought only one vehicle; there's scarcely room to park two. But Giuliani wouldn't be Giuliani if he couldn't solve a problem like that. One of the cars will have to be parked over his 'garage pit', a ditch dug in the ground with concrete ramps on either side. The other can park at an angle on the side of the hill. It means, of course, we can't use our roof tents.

We take a look around the Mission and it's not just we three Europeans but our African drivers too who're amazed that anyone can live here. When we put it to the priest, he answers with a laugh: 'I go where the Samburu are and where there's water. Those are the only criteria. I don't need anything else. Of all the places I've come to know in all my years in Kenya this is the most beautiful and has the best water.' His face positively lights up with pride.

Now it's time to start unloading his vehicle. When I see two huge canisters full of diesel emerge from under the tarpaulin I can't imagine how he's going to get them to the ground. But that's no problem for Giuliani: he's put together a makeshift crane for jobs like this and a couple of the Samburu give him a hand. After that they unload enormous numbers of tins of fat for the local population and store them in a sort of shed. I watch all of this and gradually the realization dawns on me: 'This is all you have as a supply store?' But Giuliani laughs out loud and says: 'No, Corinne. This is my house. I live here. At night I throw a mattress on the table and sleep on it. It's perfectly comfortable.' He can see I can hardly believe my eyes and adds: 'It's all I need.' While we're talking another Italian priest wanders up to join us. He's seventy-seven years old and lives here with Giuliani but comes across as extremely sprightly.

Later we go to see the focal point of the Mission, the most original church I've ever seen. It looks more like a giant *manyatta*. It's a circular building with the roof and side walls covered with blue, yellow and green sheets of plastic with a few bits of straw sticking out between them. The front doors are made of corrugated iron and are opened vertically and supported by posts. Inside this round tent are planks nailed onto wooden stakes about fifteen inches off the ground. These are the pews. Giuliani is visibly proud of his church and tells us tomorrow we'll see it full.

Now it's time to sort out sleeping arrangements. I get a little corrugated iron shed for myself while Albert and Klaus have to share another one. Because the ground slopes so much there's nowhere for the drivers to erect their tent, but Giuliani has a solution to this too. He offers to let them sleep on the open back of his Unimog truck, under the tarpaulin. It ought not to be a problem for one night.

We've barely finished putting our things away when he comes round with a tray of espresso coffee – very Italian! Then he asks us into his little kitchen, showing us on the way his little vegetable garden with a magnificent shrub with red flowers at the gate. He's planted all sorts of vegetables, including tomatoes, aubergines and lettuce, and there are plants of all sorts growing inside and outside the little garden fence. We go into the modest kitchen, which contains a tall fridge that runs off solar power, like all the Mission lighting. They cook on bottled gas. On the table is a big chunk of Italian hard cheese, salami and ham. How on earth does he conjure up all these delicacies out here at the ends of the earth?

He's forever running around, scarcely taking time to sit down for a minute. As he is the cook here it'll be up to him to prepare our evening meal, something simple but good. 'We don't have the fine things you see on the table there every day, you know,' he says with a wink, pouring red wine into our coffee cups. That's the way he is: simple, uncomplicated and a genius at organization! He exudes so much energy you automatically feel in good hands, Giuliani's mere presence works like a tonic!

Over dinner Albert asks him if he's read my book. 'Oh yes,' he replies with a smile. 'I read most carefully the things Corinne wrote: I found it particularly interesting to read that I slammed the door in her face.' With that he gets up to act out the scene of our first meeting when he sent me away rather rudely and has everyone in stitches of laughter. But at least he confirms that what he read in the book does indeed fit perfectly with what he recalls of the occasion. He goes on to say that as far as he was concerned my love for Lketinga couldn't last because the Samburu see marriage and sexuality very differently from the way we do in Europe.

After telling us about the terrible Turkana attack he goes on to explain about a new risk to the region. It seems the government wants to turn the whole area between Barsaloi and Sererit into a wildlife reserve. The natives have been promised jobs in the tourism industry but they would lose something far more important: the right to run their own part of the country. They would no longer be able to find enough pasture-land for their herds. Giuliani is convinced they can only survive out here as long as they and their herds can maintain their semi-nomadic lives.

He talks himself up into an absolute rage at the idea these people could have their land taken from them. Here in Sererit it would be particularly cruel because they have clean fresh water flowing down from the mountain all year round. He gets a map out to explain it all to us.

Fascinating as his conversation is, I have to ask the whereabouts of the toilet. Giuliani points out a tiny hut made of straw and plastic sheeting. As soon as I go in I have to burst out laughing. Out here too of course, it's simply an earth closet. But with a difference! There's a wooden frame around the hole in the ground but on top of it two tree branches, carefully bent to shape, make up the toilet seat. Back to nature with a vengeance! There's a shower next to it, which works on the same principle as the one on the film set. And there's even a separate water tap so you can wash your hands under running water. I'm so impressed I go back to join the company, singing the praises of the sanitary facilities. As soon as I open my mouth, however, they all start laughing out loud. When I stare at them in amazement they tell me Giuliani had predicted I would come back enchanted by his toilet facilities, as he'd made the seat especially for me.

While the men continue to laugh amongst themselves about Giuliani's 'little room' I hear the tinkle of bells and look behind the house to see a few

Chance meeting with a Samburu woman at the river

James's new house

Morning in the corral

Milking a goat with Lketinga's sister

The herd seeking shade from the midday sun

Our old shop in Barsaloi

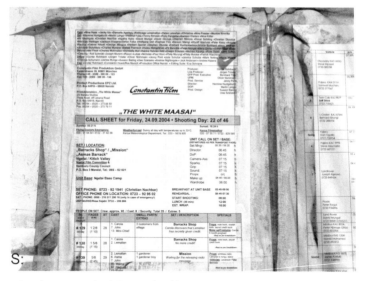

The shooting schedule on the film set

In the reconstruction of a Samburu village

Face to face with Nina Hoss, the film's leading lady

Jacky Ido, who plays Lketinga in the film

Father Giuliani's new church in Sererit

With Father Giuliani and Klaus at the Mission

Sunday mass in Sererit

Listening to Father Giuliani

Chance meetings with old friends

Mama Natasha with her latest child

Lketinga shows off his new blanket

Morning outside Lketinga's *manyatta*

With Mama and Lketinga's sister outside their *manyatta*

The going away party

A family photo with Albert, my publisher

With my African family

Making me feel welcome again

With James, Stefania and Little Albert

Mama and I, together

Fond farewells, with Mama and Lketinga

The hospital in Wamba where I gave birth to Napirai

At the door of my hospital room

With the Flying Doctors, in Nairobi

The Likoni ferry, where it all began

black and white cows coming slowly back home. Behind them two warriors and a girl are looking up at us with quiet curiosity. It has to be rare that they have white people coming to visit them out here in the bush. I'm feeling fidgety and decide to go and have a little look around the Mission grounds. On my tour I'm surprised to come across a warrior in the garden, decked out in full traditional style with strings of coloured beads around his naked shoulders and a bush knife by his red loincloth. But what surprises me is the thing he's holding in his right hand: a green watering can. He pays no attention to me, concentrating solely on the business of carefully watering the garden.

Giuliani tells me later the Samburu often help him in the garden. He pays them for it to get them used to the idea of doing jobs they don't see the purpose of or simply aren't used to. The Samburu even helped him erect the simple Mission and school buildings and make the road. He sees his first job here as making life better for people, whether it's by teaching them about hygiene and diseases or building schools and helping them to make something more of their lives. In this remote district he fulfils the roles of teacher, employer, friend, adviser and helper all in one.

The Samburu in the garden is almost the only person I come across in my little stroll and I begin to get the impression that there's no one actually living here. But, as everywhere in the bush, as soon as you think you're certain there's nobody else around another human being pops up as if from nowhere. I spend a while just taking in this wild romantic landscape before going back to join the others in Giuliani's kitchen to help with the evening meal. But all I'm allowed to do is chop up onions and tomatoes for the salad; he's doing all the cooking himself.

All at once the silence is broken by the unmistakable tones of Italian opera. It hits me completely out of the blue and despite the heat I find myself coming out in goose bumps. The music seems so anomalous in this harsh, remote part of the world that it's almost as if it's from another planet. Giuliani notices my astonishment and bursts spontaneously into song along with the music. Klaus and Albert stick their heads in too to see what's going on. It turns out the source of the music is a solar-powered CD-player.

Before long we're all sitting down around big plates of garlic spaghetti. To go with it there are chunks of goat meat roasted in a metal pan. It all tastes wonderful and over dinner our host starts telling us about what he plans to do next. Apart from anything else, when he gets enough money he wants to build a bigger church because the existing one is no longer big enough, as he assures us we'll see at mass tomorrow. After that he'd like to lay down a track all the way from here to Barsaloi because at present he has to make a huge detour when the rains come and the river is impassable. This becomes a big problem, particularly when someone is ill or there's been an accident and he's in a hurry.

During the course of outlining his future plans he remembers a story about my life with Lketinga that we then tell Albert and Klaus between us. Initially the older priest listens too but then he suddenly gets up and leaves the kitchen saying he doesn't want to miss the news from Italy. We give Giuliani a puzzled look and he explains that there's an Italian radio station to be heard at the same time every evening.

A little later we all wander out into what has now become a beautiful starry night and find the old priest sitting on a chair with a little radio pressed against his ear. It's a moving scene. We sit ourselves down on the free chairs while Giuliani fetches an iron bed frame and quite calmly lays down on it to point out various star constellations to us. This is their evening ritual, the two of them out here while the older man listens to the radio and then they chat or watch the stars together. By eight o'clock they are normally in bed.

While we're listening to Giuliani's tales I spot tiny flickering flames on the far hillside, almost certainly from the cooking fires of the distant *manyattas*. Now and then human voices drift across to us on the wind. Everything is calm and peaceful. Giuliani, however, can't keep still for more than ten minutes before he jumps up to do something else. I take the opportunity to pinch his place on the iron bed frame and look straight up at the stars. There's a full moon surrounded by a bright halo and the stars look so low you could almost reach up and grab them. It's one of those moments when I feel completely at one with nature, an absolute high!

Giuliani comes back and asks with a laugh: 'Corinne, do you like the bed? I made it myself. If you like, you can sleep out here on it. I do it myself sometimes.'

I don't have to be asked twice. How can I refuse? I fetch my thin mattress, sleeping bag and a couple of blankets and make myself up a comfy bed on the iron frame. My two companions look at me somewhat sceptically and Klaus says: 'You're not serious! You really intend to sleep out here? You don't know what sort of creatures might come prowling around!'

'It's not a problem, Klaus. This is something I have to do. Spending a night out here in the open will compensate for not spending one in Mama's *manyatta*,' I reply happily.

Before we retire for the night we take it in turns to visit the 'bathroom', equipped with a torch of course. The drivers climb under the tarpaulins on the back of the lorry and Albert and Klaus disappear into their 'tin can'. I slide down inside my sleeping bag, pull the blankets over me and pull the hood of my tracksuit over my head to avoid getting cold during the night. It feels so wonderful I could sing out loud! I feel as if I've reached the ends of the earth; I feel free as a bird, light as a feather and infinitesimal in the face of the universe. All the problems I imagine in my life seem suddenly meaningless and unimportant. I stare up into the heavens, recognizing more and more constellations. On the distant horizon behind a dark hill suddenly a light appears, blinking on and off and then I realize that it's an airplane flying 33,000 feet above me to some distant location.

Giuliani potters around in his kitchen for a little while longer before turning the light out. I can hear the drivers talking to each other in their own language for a bit and then finally everything is quiet. My thoughts return to my family in Barsaloi and I wonder how tomorrow's party will go and how many people will turn up. Almost immediately afterwards it will be time for us to leave. But I put this thought to the back of my mind, not to let it dampen my mood.

Here and there I can hear rustling noises in the undergrowth but it doesn't worry me: my bed is three feet off the ground. The air is pure and cool and as tiredness gradually overcomes me I give thanks in a silent prayer that so far my return to Africa and reunions with friends and family in Barsaloi and here in Sererit have gone so well. In the middle of the night I suddenly wake up. My nose is cold, the blankets have slipped off the bed and there's a kitten sleeping on them. I make my little nest up again, this time with the kitten purring next to me. In the distance I can hear the roar of a bigger cat: possibly a lion or a leopard, it occurs to me, but I fall asleep again anyway. The next morning Giuliani tells me that it was indeed one of the relatively numerous leopards who still live around here.

Divine Service in the Ndoto Mountains

Today is not just Sunday but also Albert's birthday. Of course he tries to hide the fact and of course he doesn't get away with it. I've made sure of that. At breakfast we're already singing 'Happy Birthday' with Giuliani's strong voice dominating all the others. Then the priest has to get ready for mass, which leaves the rest of us with an hour to kill. Klaus grabs his camera equipment and we set out along the track on which the cows came home the previous night. Before long we arrive at the dried-up river bed that runs between the magnificent rocks. Klaus and I decide this is the best spot to capture Albert's birthday for posterity. We sit down on the rocks and Klaus films me handing him his birthday present. After all, not everyone can say they've celebrated a birthday on a dried-up river bed deep in the African bush and opened a present bought on Bahnhofstrasse in Zürich. Albert is rather touched and we all have a laugh together.

But as ever we discover that even this little birthday ceremony attracts attention: no sooner have we sat ourselves down than a couple of children pop up out of the ground and sit a few feet away watching us without expression. It's half an hour before their attention wavers and they gradually steal silently away.

We arrive back at the Mission with the first churchgoers. Almost all of them are women and girls in traditional dress. Most have children with them. First of all the little ones are given a cup of *utschi* – runny maize porridge – and then they and their mothers sit down on the benches in the church. More and more people arrive to fill up the *manyatta*-church. Some of them stop for a moment and give us – particularly Klaus with all his photographic equipment – scowls; others, however, pay next to no attention to us. Most of the children are wearing just a simple red school skirt, but the women have done themselves up and are wearing their best clean brightly coloured kangas. Their faces are glistening from the fat they've rubbed into them and they have coloured headbands around their foreheads. Some even have the giraffe-hair necklaces, which are seen more and more rarely these days and normally only worn at big festivals.

However, if seems that for these women coming to church on Sunday is a festival in its own right. They sing and clap along to the wonderful African hymns with such joyful gusto that it warms the heart. The hymns are accompanied by a little drum and two tambourines made out of willow branches and labels from bottles. The songs are all rhythmic and lively and some of the women get so carried away that they bob up and down with their heads just like they do during the traditional dances. Most of them sing out loud and clear and all of them are in tune. This all goes on until Father Giuliani comes out with a metal box, takes his altar cloth out of it and spreads it on an ordinary table. He lays this simple altar table with a coloured cloth and sets down a chalice of wine and the salver with the host on it.

By now this round hut, identifiable as a Christian church only by virtue of a simple wooden cross and a few paper pictures of Mary and the baby Jesus, is absolutely packed. There are even a few old men in the back row, which says something for Father Giuliani. To get a Samburu man into church takes some doing. In between the hymns Giuliani speaks to them in Swahili, which is simultaneously translated into Maa by one of the Samburus. Towards the end of the mass the host is dispensed and another hymn sung. Then in conclusion everyone shakes hands with their neighbour. I look at the striking faces of the women present and gather that coming to church like this is not just a change of routine but a genuine pleasure. The mass over, Giuliani puts his altar cloth and vessels away while his translator hands out chewing tobacco to the elders for their journey home. As a church service, this was for us an impressive experience that will leave a lasting memory.

Going-Away Party

But now it really is time to be heading back to Barsaloi. After a long drive we approach the outer suburbs of Baragoi, the main town of the Turkana. I can't help thinking of the unprovoked attack that took place a few years ago. It was from here that the Turkana set out to attack the Samburu. We turn off the road just before we get to the main settlement and all at once it starts bucketing with rain. We can hardly see the surface of the road under a brown river rushing towards us. Luckily this is just the earliest stage of the rainy season and the ground is still extremely dry so it doesn't immediately turn to mud and we can drive on. I only hope it isn't raining in Barsaloi or else we're going to have problems getting enough fires going to cook all the food for the party. Giuliani reassures me but says it will definitely hit the film crew down at Wamba.

After a long slow journey on the wet tracks we pass the place where Lketinga and I, years ago, got stuck with a dead car battery. It took Lketinga several hours to run back to ask Giuliani for help while I waited out here in the scorching heat alone with a baby. Four hours in all! But all that came by was a herd of zebras and a few ostriches. Giuliani remembers the occasion and shakes his head and laughs: 'Now, Corinne, that wasn't the only time I had to get you out of a fix!'

Soon after, we reach Barsaloi and to my relief it's cloudy but there's been no rain. Father Giuliani has to hurry, though, if he's still to get across the potentially dangerous Wamba River. We agree to meet up for one last meal in Kenya together in Nairobi, say our goodbyes and he sets off towards Wamba at high speed.

The drivers are already fixing up the sleeping accommodation at the parking spot next to the Mission. We head over to the corral where there are already lots of party guests waiting for us. James looks obviously relieved to see us: 'Thank God, you're back. We've been cooking all day and there's masses of food. The first guests arrived this morning already and everybody's starving. But I told them there'd be no food until you got back!' I ask how Lketinga's been and find he's been working hard. He and his older brother have slaughtered four goats between them and divided up all of the meat to be cooked at the various huts.

As we enter the corral I feel almost overwhelmed. People come running up to me from all sides calling out as ever: '*Supa, Mama Napirai, seian a ge?*' I shake hands all round and get spat on in blessing a few times. Most of them I recognize at least by sight. There are three dozen women clustered around Mama's hut alone waiting patiently. I only get to greet Mama by shaking her hand like all the others. I'm pleased to see, however, that she's wearing her new flowery coloured skirt. She's sitting with her daughter by the door to the hut smiling happily.

James suggests we get on with dishing out the food. Before long the goats will be coming home and then the women will all have work to do. Nonetheless, according to tradition, the men have to eat their fill before the women can start. We're a bit embarrassed that everything's been ready for hours but they've been waiting for us to get here.

Lketinga is wearing his new red shirt. He takes my arm and leads me into one of the rooms in James's house where giant platters laden with boiled rice, beans and meat are laid out. I'm very impressed by the lengths they've gone to. It looks like enough food to feed five hundred. Papa Saguna stands by the door where there's a queue of men with plates. Lketinga has a brief word with him to say it's time to start. His brother takes enormous pains to make sure the food is all served out properly, while Lketinga tells me how they were busy all day getting things ready so our guests could really enjoy the party. I'm astounded by what they've managed to lay on and how smoothly everything goes.

We Europeans, however, find ourselves standing around looking lost as it all looks more like a charity food handout than a party. When I lived here the parties were different. Because we lived outside the village all the parties took place on the open savannah and the guests sat and ate in little groups spread out picturesquely across the landscape. Then when they had eaten their fill, they lined up in groups of the same age to dance to rhythmic singing, and there was a kind of magic in the air.

Today, however, the family and their corral are integrated into the village and the meal is being served inside the four walls of a house, and it doesn't look like there's going to be any dancing. Perhaps it's because this is a leaving party rather than a wedding feast or the celebration of a birth or some other more joyous occasion.

I go back to Mama's *manyatta* and sit down on the ground between her and her daughter. She's dandling Saruni on her lap with a serious look on her face. Different women keep coming up to me for a chat, some of them asking if I'm now coming back to stay with my '*lepayian*', my husband. Others, understandably, want to hear news of Napirai. Some of them suggest I should bring her back here and both of us should stay for good. I can hardly tell these good-natured souls that my daughter has become so Swiss she would almost certainly hate it here. Instead I tell them that the next time I come to visit she may well come with me to find out more about her African roots.

The women are by and large happy to sit and wait patiently until it's their turn to eat. James comes over and at least hands out some chewing tobacco. For a laugh I put my hand out too, but when I put the bitter stuff in my mouth, there's a great commotion. Mama makes it abundantly clear with energetic gestures that I should spit it all out immediately. Lketinga's sister spits on the ground next to me and tells me to do the same. I don't understand what all the fuss is about as virtually everybody else is chewing away at the stuff. James tells me it'll give me stomach problems. Apart from anything else, I'm still too young: only the old women chew tobacco. I don't really understand any of this there and then and it's only later in the hospital in Wamba that I find out more. But I do what I'm told and spit it all out on the ground. Some of them laugh and clap their hands but a few of them give me dirty looks.

One woman in particular grabs my attention because I'm certain I've never seen her before. Her shaven head is unusually shiny in the sun, her eyes are set wide apart and there are two sharp vertical lines in her forehead between her eyebrows. Her lips are puckered closed. She reaches out her hand to me, however, as if she's known me for years and asks after Napirai, her eyes twinkling almost maliciously. There are really nasty vibes coming from this woman. There's something about her aura I don't like and I make an excuse of getting up to go and see how long it'll be before the women can finally get to eat. On the way to the house I spot Lketinga's young wife with two other girls behind Mama's *manyatta*. She watches me with interest. I wonder what on earth's going on in her head.

Lketinga is keeping careful watch over the shrinking queue of waiting men. James asks me to come into the house so that at last we too can eat. But I don't want to start until the other women present are allowed to. I've spotted a few of the men already queuing up for seconds. I ask James rather tetchily when it'll finally be the turn of the women and children, who've been sitting there looking on for more than an hour already, all with their plates in their hands. James says simply: 'It'll be the turn of the women when all the men have had enough.' I'm starting to get angry now because the goats will be coming back soon and then the women won't have time to eat. I go over to stand next to Lketinga to see if I can get him to have some sympathy for the women. '*Pole, pole* – slowly, slowly,' he says in an attempt to calm me down, 'the last ones will soon have had their fill.' Then he goes over and has a word with his older brother.

They really are doing their best, but I'm a woman and I would like to see the women and children eat their fill too. I glance into the dining room and see three men sitting around the pots feeding their faces. The concrete floor is littered with gnawed bones. I'm relieved to see, however, that there's enough left. At last the final few men leave the room and Lketinga calls the women over. Immediately there's a great line of women heading in our direction. But they all form a queue without any fuss and wait their turn patiently. Then when they have filled their plates they stand around the chicken coops to eat on their feet, feeding bit and pieces all the time to the little children carried on their backs. The women chew the food first to soften it to a pulp, which they then pop into the hungry little mouths. I had to feed Napirai like that too once upon a time, as there was no such thing as baby food out here. I notice that any children who join the queue are chased away. When I mention it to James he tells me: 'It's up to their mothers to fetch food for them and they have to wait so that one family doesn't get a double portion and another nothing at all.'

I wander around looking at happy satisfied faces everywhere. All of a sudden the man who pointed out Lketinga's wife to me appears in front of me to say what a great success the party is, as so many people, particularly among the older people, have turned up. Apparently even the woman who practices the so-called 'female circumcision' is there, which is considered a great honour as she's held in high respect. I realize he's indicating the woman who made such an evil impression on me in Mama's *manyatta*. So she's the one who inflicts so much suffering on young girls in the name of tradition. Now I understand why I had such a negative reaction on meeting her. I feel a shiver run down my spine at the thought that in different circumstances a woman like her might be mutilating my daughter.

There are still woman queuing up when the goats arrive back a little while later. Things all get a bit chaotic in the corral as it fills up with animals and some of the women and girls hurry off home with their full plates so they can get on with their work. I reckon it's time for me to go back to the house and get something to eat now, when once again my 'informant' pops up to tell me Lketinga's wife wishes to shake my hand. I'm curious so I go with him.

She's standing with two other girls beside the half-finished *manyatta*. I hold out my hand to her and say '*Supa*' as a hello. She giggles in embarrassment and hides half her face behind her hand. The man says something to her and she reaches out her hand to me shyly. I'm probably the first white person she's ever touched. Her plumpish face still looks like that of a child. I say hello to the other two young girls and my 'informant' tells me they too are already married.

I'm really shocked by this. One of the girls is a whole head smaller than Lketinga's wife and looks no older than twelve at most. I let the man know how shocked I am and he says: 'Yes, it's crazy but she belongs to that man over there.' But before I can work out whom he means I see Lketinga charging over towards us with an angry expression. But before I can work out what he's so upset about, he's already cursing at us, giving a right mouthful to his wife too. She turns her head away in shame while I try to calm him down, saying I was really pleased to get to know his wife. But he won't listen and insists that I don't talk to her anymore: no good will come of it. I stomp off to James's house in annoyance, with absolutely no idea what could have got Lketinga so worked up.

James is chatting with Albert and Klaus. His wife is standing a little way away from them while Saruni clings to her father. There's no sign of Little Albert. When we ask where he is, James lays a finger on his lips and says: 'Can anyone hear a little bell tinkling?' We all listen hard and then realize it's Little Albert playing outside in the dark. We have to laugh when James tells us that they attach a bell to the toddler's foot when he goes out so it's easier to find him.

Stefania fetches a big pot of chunks of meat and sets it on the table. We all tuck in, James taking care to point out the best bits to us. By now we're chewing at the meat on the bone too. There's rice and beans to go with it.

In a while Papa Saguna comes in and sits down with us, filling a plate for himself. He never sits on a chair, just hunkers down, leaning back against the wall. Normally he's very quiet but when he does speak he gets quite animated. It seems as if now he's telling some good stories about the preparations for the party. At the end of his account he spits on the floor, like an exclamation mark! Everybody has a funny tale of their own to tell now and there's a real party mood in the house. When Klaus and Albert say they've had enough to eat after just a couple of pieces of meat each there's a gale of astonished laughter from the brothers.

As we're trying to tell them about our visit to Father Giuliani, I suddenly remember my little tape recorder, which I used to record the magnificent singing during the mass. I turn it on and everyone pricks up their ears.

Little Saruni's perked up and comes over to me, pressing the recorder to her ear in delight, her head nodding along with the music. She even manages to get her shy brother Little Albert to put the thing to his ear and we all sit there entranced watching the pair of them, his little eyes growing ever bigger and rounder.

Only Lketinga puts a bit of a damper on things, sitting there saying hardly a word. I get the feeling he's already thinking about our departure because he keeps giving me long, penetrating looks. Suddenly out of the blue he asks: 'What time are you leaving tomorrow?'

'As soon as we've done our packing we'll go in to see the priest in the Mission to say farewell and then come down to the corral to drink tea with Mama.'

'Okay, no problem, Mama wants to give you her blessing and that of *Enkai* [the Samburu word for God]. I will come with you as far as Maralal.'

I'm surprised and delighted to hear this because it means we can stretch out the goodbyes.

By now Stefania and the children have already retired to the bedroom, and it's nearly time for us to go back up the track to the Mission because we're all tired. Somehow it seems to me there was not much of a party spirit to the evening, even though the guests all seem to have had a good time and are keen to tell so.

We talk over our plans for the remainder of our trip. Albert has to head to Nairobi from where his flight leaves in two days' time. I want to spend another week in Kenya, however. There seems little point in going back to visit the film set, and as it looks as if the rains might be starting any minute, we decide to all go to Nairobi together tomorrow. The only other place I absolutely want to revisit is the hospital in Wamba where I was admitted on several occasions and where they saved my life when it was hanging by a thread. It was also the place where my beloved daughter Napirai came into the world. I want to take a few photos to bring back to her. She was the first mixed-race child to be born in Wamba. My companions understand why I want to go there and so we map out a route to Nairobi that goes via Wamba.

Dancing In The Moonlight

While we're making our plans for the next day we catch the sound, faint at first then growing louder, of hands clapping and people singing. It sounds like warriors dancing somewhere nearby. All of a sudden my tiredness is blown away and I suggest we go out to try to find them, to give Albert and Klaus the opportunity to see this typical dancing at first hand. I wrap a thick blanket around myself to keep me warm and to provide a bit of anonymity. The last thing we want to do is interrupt them. But when we reach the Mission gate we discover to our amazement that it's locked. We had no idea we were locked in at nights. Disappointed, I'm about to give up and head back to the tents when all of a sudden Albert discovers a touch of the warrior in him and, despite the late hour, goes knocking on the Mission house door. It works: they open up the main gate for us so we have a chance to see the dancing. Back in the old days I watched many dances like this and every time I found myself absolutely entranced by these slim, gracious male bodies leaping high into the air amid stamping feet, their rhythmic singing and clapping of hands.

We run through the moonlit village in the direction of the singing and after a few minutes reach an area of flat ground where the little group has assembled. We sit down under a thorn tree so as not to be recognized and interrupt things. There are just a few girls and young men and quickly realize that these are 'boys' – that is still uncircumcised and therefore not yet with the status of 'warrior'. This could lead to complications tomorrow, because as a woman 'married' to a former warrior, it's not right for me to watch uncircumcised boys dance, but I'm too carried away by the magic of their movement to care. Albert and Klaus seem equally entranced by the theatrical display before their eyes.

I remember those exciting, marvellous days when Lketinga was still a strong, handsome warrior, the tallest of all of them and the one who leaped the highest, with his long red braided hair flying in the wind. After hours of dancing the warriors looked wild and unapproachable, some of them falling into a sort of trance. These boys here are a long way from that, having just begun to learn the traditional dance.

Unfortunately it's not long before we're spotted and we hear the word '*mzungu*'. A few of them come over to say hello, while others keep dancing, but a few of them drift off. Not wanting to disturb them, we take ourselves off, but it was a fine way to end the party.

It's only a little bit later, lying in my tent, that it really comes home to me that this is our last night here. It takes forever to get to sleep and inevitably I shed a few tears. I can only hope I don't start crying again tomorrow when it's time to say goodbye.

Hard Farewells

The next morning the drivers start getting everything together while we go into the Mission to see the priest. He shows us the Samburu jewellery that the women who work in the project he runs together with James have made. As the sale of the jewellery already brings in more or less enough to feed the women and their families it means there is more left over from charitable donations for the priest to spend on hard luck cases in Barsaloi or special projects such as installing new water standpipes. Things that benefit everybody. It's good to see that money given to charity ends up in good hands here. He tells us that we're welcome to come back any time and hopes someone will let him know when the film comes out as it's bound to interest people. We promise to keep in touch and do what we can from Europe to support his work here. We thank him for his hospitality, shake hands warmly and head off.

Down in the corral, Lketinga is sitting outside Mama's *manyatta*, all ready for his journey. We crawl into the hut and once again James sits down next to me to help me say a few things to Mama. I don't know when or even if I'll ever see her again. At first we talk about things we've been through together and one old story leads to another. Amongst other things that come back to me is the time during the great rainstorm when Mama stood outside holding on to her hut to stop it being swept away by the winds and the floodwater. James translates for me and Mama laughs softly. Lketinga adds that he remembers the great flood well and the two children whose lives he saved. Old stories keep coming back to us, one after another.

Eventually James says Mama wants to give us her blessing so that our lives will be preserved and our journey will come to a happy conclusion. As the oldest of the family, Mama rises early every morning when everyone else is still asleep and gives her blessing to the whole of the corral, blessing each and every child by name. Even the goats have to be blessed so that they all come home safe and well every evening. Then she goes back to bed until everyone else gets up. When the children who look after the animals leave the corral with them they have to be blessed again. That is particularly important.

When James has finished telling us all this Mama looks at me and with a strong voice full of warmth says: 'I shall pray for you, pray that you live to be as old as I am. I shall pray for Napirai. Give her all our love and tell her my love is great. Look after her well and give her grandmother's fondest wishes to her.'

I try to memorize each and every word but find tears once again welling in my eyes. Her words move me and I ask James to tell her how much I've enjoyed being able to visit her and how wonderful it's been to see everyone again. If God wills it, I hope she will still be alive when I come back with Napirai. We hold each other's hands as we talk with just the hearth between us. My voice is shaking and I find it harder and harder to get the words out. I can feel my eyes filling with tears and I try to wipe them surreptitiously, not wanting to embarrass Mama with my endless sobbing. She thanks me for my words and gives me a warm handshake. But noticing my battle to hold back my tears, she gives me a quick smile and says: 'Have a sip of tea, that'll help!' I take the cup off her thankfully. It's really hard not to cry, saying goodbye like this. Once again I ask James to make clear my tears are a sign of my deep affection for her.

As he's translating Albert and Klaus's farewell wishes, I sit there and watch Mama's face, illuminated by a ray of sunlight falling through the straw roof. The smoke from the fire mingles with the sunlight and sitting there with a baby in her arms she exudes an aura that's almost mystical. There's so much dignity and personality to this woman that I sincerely hope one day I can bring my daughter and her grandmother together. Mama is the strongest link binding our family together. The old traditions live on in her. She embodies something that everyone here respects. We are all moved and impressed by her.

We sit there for more than an hour before eventually crawling out of the *manyatta*, which has begun to get hot inside, back into the open air. Some of the women and children have gathered in the corral to say goodbye to us. I feel a tightness grip my chest; all I really want to do is burst into tears. But Klaus amuses the children again with his digital camera and takes a few last souvenir pictures.

I stand between Mama and Lketinga's sister. Both of them have long faces and the sister keeps pressing her head against my shoulder as if she too is trying to hide her true feelings. Mama is wearing her pretty flowery skirt and her new blue shawl and uses both hands to lean with great dignity on her long stick. James in his babbling way tries to cheer everyone up again before giving the sign that it's time for the blessing. We Europeans stand between him and Lketinga while Mama closes her eyes and starts praying. After every sentence we respond '*Enkai*'. Then, at the end of this little ceremony, which has had a profound effect on all of us, I embrace Mama for the last time and stare silently into her eyes. For a few seconds she presses her head against mine and says: '*Lesere, lesere* – till we meet again'.

Now it's time to say goodbye to James, Stefania, the children and Lketinga's sister. In the distance I spot my ex-husband's young wife and our eyes meet. I get the feeling she's trying to say something to me with those eyes, but what? I have no idea. I hope only that her life with Lketinga will be pleasant enough. I have come to realize once again just how funny, witty and caring he can be, when he wants to. Perhaps my visit and all the laughter we've shared will make him a bit more civil towards her. Who knows?

James tells me to send their best wishes to my mother, her husband Hans-Peter and the rest of my family and above all to Napirai.

On our short walk to the car people thrust out their hands to shake and call '*Lesere*, Mama Napirai, *lesere*'.

As we drive slowly out of the village, people on either side of the road wave to us. I'm overcome by a feeling of sadness and pleased that at least Lketinga is with us so everything isn't over all at once. This visit has been like a window for me to look back through at all the emotion and excitement of my former life. Even if a lot has changed in the meantime, there are still many things that have remained the same. I didn't feel at all distant from the people here; on the contrary, it was like coming home. My African family and the other people of the village took me to their hearts like a long-lost daughter. And that's what makes it so hard to leave.

Nobody in the car says a word. Lketinga sits looking straight ahead and seems somehow older and gaunter. It worries me because I recall how just a couple of days ago he took Albert to one side and confided in him: 'Albert, I have really changed my life. I'm happy now.'

When we get to Opiroi, Lketinga suddenly points to a group of women and children and says: 'Look, it's Mama Natasha, don't you want to stop and say hello?' Of course I do! We used to visit one another often and it was on one of those visits that I gave her daughter the name Natasha. Her husband is Lketinga's half-brother and I liked him a lot too: we could laugh together for hours. He knew absolutely nothing at all about the 'white people's world', thought cigarette lighters were surreal and called them 'burning hands', had never drunk Coca-Cola and was suspicious of its brown colour. When he tasted his first fizzy sip he spat it out as far as he could in disgust!

Mama Natasha comes up with a little baby in her arms and calls out, '*Supa*, Mama Napirai!' I throw my arms around her in mutual delight. Natasha had told her I was here. I ask how her husband is and she tells me he's out with the cattle. The first thing she wants to know is news of Napirai. I have to show her how big my daughter is now and when she hears the Napirai goes to school she reaches out her youngest baby to me and says with a laugh: 'Here, take this lad and put him in a school too.' We all laugh. Lketinga translates for me that she now has seven children and they're all doing well. I get the impression that she has a happy marriage, her husband always seemed so good-natured and he's never taken a second wife.

The other women standing around Mama Natasha are all carrying babies in kangas on their backs. One of them is dressed in a tanned cowhide. A couple of old men come up to say hello and ask if I remember them. I nod, to please them, and they bless me with their spittle. Before we go on I dig out my two favourite kangas from my luggage and give them to Mama Natasha. She's surprised and thanks me several times over, but I'm just pleased to have met another friend before we leave.

Our journey takes us past the half-finished 'termite-church' again and then up into thickly forested country. We're shaken and thrown all over the place by the condition of the track. When it really rains here this track must rapidly get swept away and become impassable.

Just outside Maralal we make a brief stop as already we can see the rain in the distance. It's grown markedly colder. Lketinga says a few sentences for his daughter Napirai on my tape recorder. No sooner has he finished speaking than a torrential downpour breaks. We scramble for the cars and head for Maralal as fast as we can, before the road turns into a mud bath. Before long there are streams of water running towards us. The animals we come across stand there motionless in the flood of water pouring down on them, while people scurry for shelter under the trees. Our drivers have to be careful now to avoid the water-filled potholes because you can no longer see how deep they are.

In Maralal we aim to have a meal with Lketinga in one of the locals' restaurants. I suggest the Somali restaurant because I have fond memories of it.

After my first bout of malaria I could scarcely eat anything for four weeks and was nearly dead of exhaustion. The seriousness of my illness was beyond anything the doctors in the Maralal hospital could cope with, and they doubted if I'd survive the journey to the much better one in Wamba. Not knowing what to do, Lketinga and my girlfriend Jutta carried me out to the Somali restaurant. It was their last hope and it worked. The meal of cooked liver with tomatoes and onions that was set in front of me was the first thing I managed to eat, albeit in tiny mouthfuls. It turned out to be the first step on my road to recovery.

We park right outside and when we walk through the door I'm astounded how big the place has become. It's also extremely busy. Lketinga pulls the hood of his jacket over his head, like he always used to do if he didn't want to be recognized. He asks me what I want to eat and passes on the order. Unfortunately liver is no longer on the menu, so I order goat meat with potatoes and sweet tea. Lketinga orders just naan bread and tea.

I can't help wondering why he's eating so little, and he keeps looking uneasily around him. It's not exactly easy to find the right words to say goodbye in a place like this, and the two of us sit there more or less silently, even though our last few minutes together are flying by.

I ask him what it is he wants to do here in Maralal. He says he want to go to the bank to see if the money the film people promised him has been paid in. I try to say a few more personal words to him: 'Lketinga, please look after yourself. Don't start drinking again. I'm so pleased that in the last few days you haven't touched a drop. I can see how you've changed your life and it makes me really happy. I'm going to tell Napirai, and one of these days she'll come with me to Barsaloi.'

He just looks at me and says: 'Okay, I will wait for you.'

It's time to go and we leave the noisy bar. Outside it's pouring down and Maralal is sinking into the mud. All around people are taking shelter, waiting for the rain to stop. How can I say goodbye to Lketinga properly here? To throw my arms around him, with all these strangers watching, would make him feel ridiculous. Lketinga throws a thin blanket over his hooded jacket and turns to me with a calm, serious look on his face, touches my arm and says, 'Okay, *lesere*.'

He takes his leave of Klaus and Albert briefly and without turning round disappears into the crowd. We drive off slowly and I try to spot him but in the rain so many people have thrown blankets or other bits of cloth over their heads.

I feel suddenly sad. I may not love this man anymore, but he is still the father of my daughter and that makes for a lifelong bond between us. During this visit I have gained respect for him again. That our visit was a success has been largely down to him.

Thanks to the sense of humour he and James share, I've laughed more in the last few days than in the previous six months. That's why I find saying goodbye like that almost tragic. His expressionless face told me he was sad too. But he now lives in his world and I in mine, and that's how it suits both of us. The bond between us lives on in the daughter we share.

One Last Night In Samburu Country

We intend to spend the night – our last in Samburu country – in the Safari Lodge. I take the same pretty room with the open fireplace. Outside zebras and wild boar are gathering around the watering hole despite the rain. We still have time before dinner so I decide to enjoy the luxury of a hot bath to soak away my depression. There's a slight reddish-brown tinge to the water because of the rain, but I enjoy it nonetheless; Africa is no place to be pernickety.

Just as I'm getting ready there's a knock on the door and someone says, 'Madame, I have to tell you someone is waiting for you in the restaurant.' I hurry down, filled with curiosity, to find two African men sitting in armchairs. Only when I come closer do I recognize one of them: it's the bush doctor from Barsaloi who helped me on occasion with advice and diagnoses. It's immediately clear, however, that he's taken to the bottle. He introduces his companion to me as a civil servant from Maralal. I greet the doctor, surprised to see him but, my God, how he's changed! His face has grown haggard, and he's missing a couple of teeth. I'm genuinely shocked. He admits that he's had a problem with drink for several years now. I ask after his wife and children who I used to know well. He gives me a curt answer and says he met Lketinga in Maralal, who told him we were spending the night here.

Meanwhile Albert has come down. Immediately the bush doctor starts telling Albert about all the ailments I had and how often he thought I was going to die, particularly the time he had to go with me on the 'Flying Doctor' plane to Wamba. I hadn't even realized he'd been with me on board the little emergency aircraft as I'd been far too weak to take in anything and could think of nothing but the fears I had for my unborn child. He describes the emergency evacuation that saved my life in detail, mentioning that sadly the pilot of the plane is no longer alive. I'm shocked and saddened to hear it because it was the pilot's spectacular landing out in the bush that saved both my life and that of my unborn child.

We swap stories of the old days, and I remember that he gave me a goat as a wedding present. But then inevitably, before he and his companion depart, they ask for money. He tells me he has unpaid hospital bills and doesn't know how he'll get the money to pay them. It's obvious now that that's why he came here. I give him as much as I think appropriate but it leaves a sour taste in my mouth. It's a shame how low drink has brought him.

We're the only guests again for dinner and I wonder once again how this place survives. The décor and furniture are still the same as they were eighteen years ago, simple but comfortable. Tonight, however, we all retire early. I sit by the flickering fire and wonder where Lketinga is. I really hope that he can cope with his relative wealth and that he too doesn't fall victim to drink.

Before going to sleep I'm overcome by the need to offer up a prayer for my family: 'Dear God, give Mama a long life still, care for Lketinga and his family and let him become a father again. Give James the strength to keep on being the link between our two worlds. Care too for my daughter Napirai and help her to become proud of her roots.'

The Hospital in Wamba

We set off early next morning, taking a new route so as not to have to cross the wide river outside Wamba, which by now is once again flowing with water. I do my best to absorb every fleeting image, to burn every scene indelibly into my memory. Survival here is so difficult yet the landscape and its people are almost indescribably beautiful. Just to be here is to have the magic cast its spell on you.

Our cars grind along the rutted roads towards Wamba. It takes some three hours to reach the village and we head straight for the hospital. I don't expect anybody here to remember me, especially since Father Giuliani told me the last Italian nuns left three months ago and an Indian sisterhood has taken over. It's a pity, though.

However, we do what we can to find someone who can spark a few memories for me. We explain the reason for our visit at the reception, and the Indian women are pleased to help but seem to think we're from the film crew, who apparently they're expecting tomorrow. When I tell them instead that I'm actually the one who was here fifteen years ago and it's 'only' my life story that's being filmed, they immediately offer to show us around.

The deputy head of the hospital takes time to personally show us around. Everything is much as it used to be, although in a better state of repair. I'm amazed that there are so few patients. In the old days there were queues of them waiting to be seen and all the wards were full. Sometimes I had to wait up to four or five hours with my baby before we reached the front of the queue for inoculations.

We walk down the corridors until we reach the ward I shared with Sofia, my friend at the time who was also heavily pregnant. The ward is empty, so there's no objection to me going in to look around.

It's incredible! Everything's just the way it was fifteen years ago. Even the thin white sheet on the mattress on top of the iron bed frame looks identical. There's still plaster peeling from the walls in places, and there are still the same little metal cupboards next to each bed. Just looking at them brings back the sound of cockroaches scrabbling around inside. Once when I put something edible in one of them it attracted the insects during the night. All I heard at first was the noise of something rattling on the metal. I had no idea what it was until I turned on my torch and saw to my horror the mass of black insects crawling around in the circle of light, some of them even working their way into the tiniest of cracks.

I sit myself down on 'my' bed, and a deep feeling of contentment washes over me. I used to sit here for hours on end knitting. Knitting! Me, who refused absolutely to learn knitting in school! I sat here and patiently knitted the first clothes for my unborn child. For two weeks I sat here waiting impatiently for the birth. I had had no preparation, there were no antenatal classes or exercise lessons or anything like that. I didn't even know the faintest thing about going into labour, as my mother-in-law – who amongst the Samburu would normally have explained all this – and I couldn't communicate with one another. I just told myself that young girls had babies all the time and at twenty-nine therefore I could manage it too.

My memories of this room, however, are not all happy ones. I was also in here when I had a serious attack of malaria and was connected up to drips on either side, one of them infusing blood and the other a saline solution. I went through so much in this hospital, from giving birth to narrowly escaping death, that it seems miraculous that I can be sitting here on the same bed today, so well nourished and in perfect health.

Our tour of the facilities takes us next to the isolation ward, which is a part of the hospital I also know intimately. At the moment there are building works going on so we can't go inside. Apparently they're intending to move the whole facility to another part of the hospital. However, I point out to Albert and Klaus where I spent five weeks in isolation, and watched through the window at visiting time every day by a whole passing parade of people I didn't know. I remember that terrible experience only too well. My little cell was cut off from the outside world so that I couldn't even hear a human voice or the birdsong outside, not one single noise. Nonetheless, I came out of it in the end with my health restored.

We walk slowly back and I ask our guide which diseases are most prevalent nowadays. The nun tells us: 'Burns and pregnancy complications caused by the 'female circumcision'. I see the dreadful problems caused by this tradition almost every day. Even if there aren't immediate risks, such as infection, problems arise at the very latest when they come to give birth. Some girls are married as young as ten years old and end up giving birth for the first time at twelve or thirteen. Giving birth at that age is dangerous enough, but here you have the added complication that the vagina is often scarred and has lost its elasticity. Some young women die or suffer lifelong injuries as a result. Some of them end up unable to control their bladders and as a result are thrown out of their husband's families. We come across tragic cases like that on a daily basis. Despite the fact that this 'female circumcision' is against the law in Kenya, I can see this mutilation going on for a long time, especially out in the bush where nobody pays any attention to these things and the girls have virtually no rights. As long as the custom of marrying girls off young and only after they've been 'circumcised' then it will take years for education to get through to them. It's better in the towns. But the worst thing is when an 'uncircumcised', that is unmarried, girl gets pregnant; then they try everything to abort the baby. They use the most awful methods, including pouring a brew made from chewing tobacco down the girl's throat.'

So that's why they all got so worked up at our leaving party in Barsaloi when I put some of the chewing tobacco in my mouth.

'If none of that works,' the nun says, 'then they 'circumcise' the girl, even though she's pregnant. The huge loss of blood and the gaping wound, which usually gets infected, result in the abortion of the foetus and sometimes in the death of the mother. I myself,' she adds, 'am half-Samburu, half-Kikuyu, and thank God they didn't do it to me.'

Albert asks why they carry out such a ritual which to us seems so barbaric. The nun replies that it's very difficult to give a precise answer. On the one hand, there's the sheer weight of tradition, but she thinks that the men also believe that this 'circumcision' will make their wives lose any interest in other men and become more obedient and easier to keep under their control. A lot of education is needed and she can only hope that things will improve one day. The fact that the Samburu don't carry out the most extreme form of 'circumcision' practised by certain other tribes is cold comfort under the circumstances.

I think back to the conversation we had on our own with James about this just a few days ago. It was Albert who brought it up. He told us that, despite all the changes that had taken place over recent years, not much had been done about female 'circumcision'. When we asked him what he though of it himself, he said only: 'It's such a deep-rooted tradition that it's hard to get it out of your head. Amongst us, a girl only becomes a fully-fledged woman after this operation. It's always been like that and that's the way things are likely to remain.'

We ask him if the subject isn't dealt with in school. He says, 'Yes, but it doesn't do any good. Even if a man wanted to marry an 'uncircumcised' girl, her father probably wouldn't let him. In any case it rarely happens.' When I ask him to his face what he'll do about his own girls, I can see he's not happy answering the question. Even Stefania, his own wife, was 'circumcised', despite the fact she'd had the benefit of an education. 'If my daughters find a man who doesn't insist on the 'circumcision',' he says, 'then that's all right with me. But it isn't easy to find a man like that.'

I think back to Lketinga's reaction when I told him the harm this so-called 'operation' can do to girls. He got really annoyed and could hardly believe what I was telling him. But afterwards even he began to ask himself why it continued to be done. Unfortunately, however, individuals can't do a great deal to change an ancient tradition. I feel certain his new wife has probably been 'circumcised'.

We head back towards the exit, somewhat depressed by what we've been hearing. We say thank you for the tour of the hospital and take our leave. Before I climb back into the car I take one last look around me, hardly able to believe that fifteen years ago my own 'Swiss Miss' first saw the light of day here. It seems almost unbelievable.

Tomorrow the film crew arrive here and Nina will 'give birth' to her 'baby'. But will they also put their hands over her mouth so no one can hear her scream?

Return to Nairobi

We leave Wamba and head towards Isiolo. A few miles along the way we have to make a hair-raising crossing over a raging river on a bridge with no barriers on either side. It's easy to see here the effect the rain has had up in the mountains. There's nothing but a torrent of red-brown water as far as the eye can see with just a few 'thumb palms' sticking out of it here and there. The crocodiles that normally live here are nowhere to be seen. The sky is leaden grey. It looks as if it will rain again soon.

Eventually, however, the road improves as we approach civilization. After two hours on the road we find ourselves coming into a hamlet made up of just a few wooden shacks, shops and a bar or two. At least it's a chance to stop for a tea break. As white people we're immediately taken into an area of our own, a back room where we sit ourselves down on threadbare sofas with white lacy throws on them. The bare walls are painted with animal motifs. These are all little touches designed to make the place appear more 'classy'. We order up some tea, which tastes good, although not as good as in Mama's *manyatta*. We drink it with a few biscuits and then it's time to get back on the road.

We meet safari buses coming in the opposite direction all the time now, bumping along the roads under the rain clouds. Every now and then I make out wooden signposts bearing exotic-looking names of tourist lodges. Since we left Samburu country both the people and the vegetation have changed. There's much more agriculture here. The women carry baskets filled with fruit and vegetables on their heads. There are no more of the brightly coloured Samburu kangas to be seen; most people wear European-style clothing.

We arrive in Isiolo in late afternoon and decide to spend the night there. It would be far too strenuous and probably quite dangerous to drive on over these bad roads in the dark. Isiolo is a horrid, dirty little town. I notice that there are a lot more Muslims living here now than there used to be. Our driver tells us the town is effectively divided in two, with Christians in one half and Muslims in the other, most of them of Somali origin.

We book ourselves in to one of the 'better' lodging houses and agree to meet up shortly for something to eat. After dinner we don't feel like wandering around the dark and dirty streets and instead sit and enjoy the evening air on a sort of roof terrace in the hotel. It seems as if our hotel is the place to meet for all of the well-to-do and 'powerful people' in town. The men are mostly overweight and dressed in modern suits while their plump wives wear African fashions or outsize European dresses. Life here seems a lot more bustling and modern than in Maralal or Barsaloi. I don't like it and am pleased when we leave for Nairobi the next morning.

The closer we get to the capital the more traffic there is on the roads. Everywhere you look there are people and cars. After the calm of the bush Nairobi seems horribly hectic and noisy. It seems a lot worse now than it did when we first arrived from Europe. I can hardly believe that it was only fourteen days ago. We've seen and done so much in the past two weeks that it seems a lot longer to me.

We take the rented Land Cruisers back to the safari company and thank our drivers John and Francis for their faultless services. The main and most important part of the journey is over now, but for me it's time to go back to Mombasa to draw a full circle and go back to the spot where it all began eighteen years ago.

Klaus offers us the use of the apartment here in Nairobi where he and his fiancée Irene have been living for the past two years. As Albert's flight for Munich leaves tonight we decide to make an effort to get in touch with Father Giuliani again and are delighted to find out that indeed he's staying not far from here. We agree to meet him in an Italian restaurant. Somehow I find it hard to imagine him here in Nairobi, in 'civilization'. To me, he's a pioneer, a lone wolf, anything but a city person.

Klaus lives in a quieter, more expensive part of town, where the apartment blocks are surrounded with walls and barbed wire. Only people known to the security guards are allowed in. Within the compound there's a restaurant, a gymnasium and a beauty parlour. The idea of having to go through security checks just to get to the gym seems really bizarre. Only later do I discover that even perfectly normal restaurants are fenced off and have guards on the door. In the old days only the smartest villas had this sort of security. It seems Nairobi has become a lot more dangerous. After dark nobody will even walk five minutes to a restaurant. Anyone who can afford it uses a locked vehicle to cover every yard.

It's not the sort of life I'd like to lead. People here are slaves to their property. I'd rather live in Barsaloi more or less in the open air, with next to nothing to my name and nothing that needs guarding. We didn't have to worry about thieves, just lions and hyenas.

When we get to the restaurant at the time we arranged to meet we find Giuliani roaring up the road towards us on his motorbike. He's wearing a helmet that looks pre-Second World War. It's the first time I've seen him in 'normal' clothes: long trousers, a pullover and proper shoes.

We've been joined by an elderly English couple who're involved in a big way in the Kenyan film industry so it's not long before we're talking about the *White Masai* movie project. Father Giuliani wants to know who's playing him in the film. Wagging his finger with a laugh he says, 'I'm warning you: if he's not right as me or if you've tinkered with the facts, then I'll be after your blood, wherever you're hiding.' We all laugh out loud. The name of the actor means nothing to him. But how on earth could it? He hasn't had a television for years and even if he had, there's no reception out where he lives. But maybe there'll be a movie premiere in Nairobi for the first showing in Kenya. That's always possible. He and James would almost certainly love to attend, although I'm not so sure about Lketinga.

Sadly the couple of hours we have fly by and we have to break up the party to head for the airport to see Albert off. When we get there I suddenly feel homesick for my daughter. I miss her such a lot. But there are still a few places and people that I have to see again on my 'journey into the past.'

Flying Doctors

The first thing I want to do is go and visit AMREF, the African Medical and Research Foundation. Untold people throughout Africa – besides me – owe their lives to their Flying Doctors. Apart from their emergency work, however, the organization has been working over the last fifty years on all sorts of programmes and concrete projects with the aim of setting up a basic health service over as wide an area as possible. I want to go and see them not just to thank them in person for saving my life fifteen years ago but to try and help make their work known to as many people as possible.

When Klaus and I arrive the next morning we find they're all ready and waiting for us. We're taken to see the woman in charge of the emergency air ambulance service and I'm astounded to hear from her just how much this organization has got up and running throughout Africa.

Originally they got their reputation for the 'Flying Doctors', pilots that everyone knew could land and take off even in the remotest parts of the bush. That was what was needed to rescue me in the nick of time from Barsaloi and fly me to Wamba.

But here in Nairobi they've also opened up a hospital in the biggest slum district and installed toilets and clean water facilities. I'm delighted to take up their offer to see their work on the ground. We arrange it for the following day: going into Nairobi's slums where the poorest of the poor live needs some preparation. It's not a good idea for white people to just wander around; there's every chance of being robbed, mugged or even murdered. Before we can go into the area we need a specially marked car and a driver who knows his way around. They also need to tell the hospital in advance.

Nobody objects when we ask to see the aircraft hangars so Klaus can take a picture of me next to the plane that I was rescued in. On the way there we're joined by the woman who'll take us around the Kibera slum tomorrow. Unfortunately when we get to the hangar there's only one large aircraft to be seen as all the little ones are in use. But then out on the tarmac we notice one smaller aircraft that resembles the one in which I was flown out the bush when I was so ill my life was in danger. Klaus's professional eye immediately sees that the light for taking photographs is much better out there. The plane is only about sixty feet away from us but we're not allowed onto the tarmac, as the little Wilson airfield is used not only by AMREF but also by light aircraft belonging to safari companies as well as private individuals.

As it's quiet at the moment, however, the AMREF women ask one of the policemen standing nearby if we can go over and take pictures next to the aircraft for five minutes. Normally you need official authorization, which has to be applied for in writing and can take two or three days to be granted, but the policeman just laughs and eventually says: 'Okay, you can go there.'

So we stroll over to the little rescue plane and while Klaus takes pictures the woman in charge of the air service explains the improvements they've made to their fleet. Nearby a couple of mechanics are lying in the shade of another small aircraft, having a midday nap. All of a sudden the deceptive calm is disrupted by a self-important man storming up to us in a rage. One of the AMREF women whispers, 'Uh-oh, now we're in for it. That's the security chief.'

He orders us to stop taking photographs immediately and explain ourselves. The two women explain the situation and show him their identity papers and business cards. But he is totally unimpressed by the business cards of a couple of women and insists that the tarmac is off-limits and that photographs can only be taken with written authority. The fact that there's nothing going on and that the photographs are being taken in a good cause doesn't impress him at all. He refuses even to listen to a word we say and instead insists on telling us he has the power to lock us all up in jail for years.

I can hardly believe my ears. There's not another aircraft to be seen anywhere and we're only twenty paces from the hangar. Rules are rules but we're hardly talking about an offence that merits a long jail sentence. The two women try to keep calm and make him see reason. But even the policeman who gave us permission gets put through the mill and told he's incompetent. By now we've been standing out on the tarmac in the scorching heat for at least half an hour and have run out of arguments. We're simply not sure what he wants: whether he's looking for a bribe or just trying to demonstrate his power. He's clearly every upset, however. By now a few other men have come over to join the discussion. Everybody's now staring at us and we're starting to feel like serious criminals. It's absolutely ironic: here we are trying to do something that could gain them useful publicity and a jumped-up little local official is trying to make his mind up whether or not to have us arrested.

Suddenly one of the AMREF women has a brainwave. She announces she has to be back in town for lunch with an ambassador and she's not going to be able to make it now. She has to let him know, as he is an ambassador after all. She's allowed to make the call but in fact uses the opportunity to call her boss and tell him we need someone in authority to come here and sort things out! He turns up in next to no time and asks what's going on. The security chief starts explaining our 'conduct' to him at length. There's some more discussion but before long his tone changes and we're simply told we can go – just like that! We have no idea what was said to change his mind and we're not about to ask; the main thing is that we're not about to end up in an African jail.

After that nasty experience we take ourselves off out of the building as quickly as possible and find a restaurant where we can have a drink. We've got enough to talk about now for the rest of the day.

The Kibera Slum

Next morning we meet up as arranged outside the AMREF offices. Everything is ready and we set off straight away. Before long we're approaching the sea of corrugated iron roofs that marks the beginning of the slum. Our guide tells us this is the biggest slum district in Nairobi. Some sixty percent of the city's population live in conditions like these. There are some 700,000 people squeezed into Kibera alone. The AIDS rate is sky-high and diseases such as tuberculosis spread like wildfire, particularly because the public hygiene is catastrophic. There is an average of only one toilet for every four hundred people! AMREF has built a substantial number of public sanitary facilities that charge only a small fee to cover the costs of cleaning them. That has done something to improve the situation. Before, you didn't dare even walk through this part of town without a protective cover on your head because people just did what they had to in plastic bottles or bags and hurled them out of the windows. They called these bags of excrement sailing through the air 'flying toilets'. Klaus and I exchange looks of disgust and horror.

We drive slowly along a track between makeshift market stalls selling huge quantities of clothing, bags, household goods and even brand new radios. It seems everybody has something to hawk. On either side our car is squeezed in by thickly pressed crowds of people. I feel uneasy, sitting here as a white person in a car pushing its way through this mob. But our driver tries to reassure me: 'This car is marked so that people can tell it belongs to aid workers whom they can rely on for help.'

He stops the car and we climb out. A boy from the crowd with gaps in his teeth is told to look after the car and he'll earn a few shillings. For a minute or two I feel almost suffocated by the stench. It's incredibly hot and wherever I look I see men, women, children and mountains of rubbish. This whole 'city' is made up of shacks knocked together out of wood and corrugated iron. We hop and jump over piles of waste and find ourselves crossing a railway line that runs barely two yards away from the market stalls but is barely visible beneath the children and goats cluttering the tracks. Every few steps we come across pools of stinking water. Our guide tells us we're lucky with the weather. As soon as the rains start the mud and excrement mix together into an ankle-deep sludge and the stink becomes unbearable. There are chickens pecking about in the dirty damp ruts, and it occurs to me that I wouldn't like to eat their eggs. Music belts out from behind each and every thin wooden wall.

People watch us suspiciously with blank faces. Only the children seem to have any curiosity and before long there's a merry gang of them tagging along behind us. I'm astonished to see some of them wearing pretty blue dresses. These are their school uniforms, I'm told. AMREF has even built a school here. Others, though, wear only tattered T-shirts and stand there barefoot in the dust and dirt. Many of them are covered in spots and scabs, but they beam smiles at us and say, 'Hello *Mzungu*, how are you?' I take a few of them by their little hands and ask them their names. But then they just turn shy.

We plod past the newly built toilets to make our way to a water standpipe. The water here is filtered and almost totally free of bacteria, so everyone has access to clean drinking water from the tap. Since this standpipe was installed there has been a dramatic drop in illnesses, particularly those that cause diarrhoea. On the corner of a big, empty square we come to the AMREF hospital. In the entrance hall queues of the sick wait their turn to be seen.

We're taken upstairs and introduced to several of the staff. A gaunt, elderly man starts by explaining to us how difficult it was to get the hospital up and running. Even the aid organizations find it hard to make any headway in the slum districts. People are mistrustful because they've been let down by empty promises so many times before. Over time, however, the hospital has come to be well used, and one big advance has been that more and more women are now registering to have their babies there. AMREF is also engaged in providing medical training for local people, particularly from the slum district itself, which is one more step to improving things. After an hour we leave the building with a greatly increased respect for the incredible job the people here do to help the weak and the sick.

Outside we come across a group of young people who work for AMREF after school every day. They tell us their job is a sort of reconnaissance task: they wander around the area, which they all know like the back of their hand, and keep an eye on what's going on. If they come across someone seriously ill or wounded they inform the hospital immediately so they can get help. As a rule of thumb, people here don't place too much value on human life.

On the way back to the car I spot a mother pig with her piglets rummaging in the dross around a rubbish heap. Just two yards away from me a man stands urinating on some planks. A few feet further away an old woman is crouching in a shelter grilling fish in a pan over an open fire. Next to her about fifty raw fish lie on a makeshift table swarming with flies. I've never seen so many flies before, not even at the worst of times living in a *manyatta*. It makes me sick to even think that these fish are going to be sold and eaten. The temperature is thirty-five degrees and the stink is something rotten. The toothless old woman laughs when she sees how disgusted I look and waves a piece of cardboard to fan the flames. A few paces on a man is selling five corn cobs he's grilled. I'm horrified but at the same time fascinated to see how much energy these people put into just surviving. Nobody complains; everybody just tries to muddle through as best they can.

Back at the railway tracks I decide to buy a bag for my journey from one of the women there. She's delighted to show me her selection. Naturally they're all covered with dust having been hung out all day on her wooden stall. While I'm deciding which to buy a goods train hurtles past. People leap off the tracks, and I squeeze up against the stall as hard as I can. A cloud of dust sent up by the passing train covers all the goods and flies into my face. But within a few seconds it's all over, as if it was just a fleeting phantom, and the women are shaking their goods free of the dust. To think they do this all day long, every day of their lives! Once again it brings home to me how privileged our lives are in Europe. I pay for the bag and we walk slowly back to the car. From every corner we hear the cacophony of music and voices as we drive off, slowly squeezing our way down the narrow alleyways, watched all the way by countless pairs of eyes. I feel anything but comfortable.

As we drive back I mentally compare the life of the slum-dwellers with that of my family in Barsaloi. Obviously they don't know the meaning of being 'comfortable' in our European sense, but they live in wide-open spaces with blue sky above them. Their way of life is simple and tough, but it is anything but impoverished. Here in the slum, on the other hand, these people are really the poorest of the poor. Most of them originally came from a rural environment in the hope that life in the city would be easier. But those who end up in the slum find it almost impossible to get out.

When we get back to Klaus and Irene's place I find I need to take a long, long shower. But even after that I can't get the mental images of the Kibera slum out of my head for hours. That evening I refuse to go to one of the expensive restaurants where we'd pay as much for a meal as countless people earn in a month. So instead Klaus and Irene take me to a simple Somali restaurant that's mostly used by local people. It turns out to be a much pleasanter, quiet and convivial evening, if only perhaps because the impressions of the day have at least slightly begun to fade.

Mzungu Masai

The next day we set off for the famous River Road to take another look at the Igbol, the very basic hotel in which I mostly stayed when I had to come to Nairobi. The friendly staff here always called me 'Mzungu Masai', a nickname that gave me the title for my first book. But even in my wildest dreams back then I never imagined that millions of people would later find inspiration in my *White Masai* life. On the way to the Igbol we have to pass the Nyayo Building, which I came to hate so much. How many times was I forced to come here and stand around filled with prayers, hopes and often despair? I've almost forgotten now what I needed such and such a stamp for. All I know is I expended huge amounts of nervous energy and adrenalin dealing with the bureaucrats who inhabit this building.

We find a parking space and a boy who offers to watch the car for us. First of all we take a stroll past the Stanley Hotel, a well-known spot that in the old days was patronized almost exclusively by white people sitting out on the terrace. Today it's much more mixed, and Kenyans are in the majority. I let myself swim in the sea of people, taking in every impression. The news-stand is still on the corner where it always was, but now there are five times as many different papers on display. We walk down a couple of side streets until I find the Odeon cinema, the landmark that tells me the Igbol can't be far. Even the telephone box that I used to use to call home to Switzerland is still there. The only difference is that nowadays there is no longer a queue outside it as even in Nairobi people all have mobile phones.

But I search in vain for the entrance to the restaurant that I remember used to adjoin the hotel, and where the reception and cash desk used to be there is now only a fast-food counter. The big communal dining room where backpackers from all over the planet used to meet up is gone, and with it the charm that used to make this place special.

My curiosity both satisfied and disappointed, we walk on. The streets are chaotic and noisy with *matatus* honking their horns continually as their drivers tout for custom. There's music coming from almost every bar or shop, and neon advertisements in the most garish colours on every wall. Here and there people in rags or with disabilities hold their hands out to beg for money. This is Nairobi at its most hectic, noisy, shrill and in your face. I remember dragging my heavy bags around here with a baby on my back and realize I can no longer imagine it.

Klaus suggests we go and take a look at the Masai market. I agree with delight, realizing that when I fled the country fourteen years ago I didn't even have a chance to take any souvenirs with me. Now I have a chance to make it up. It doesn't take long to get there by car, and the expansive market with all the colourful goods and attractive Masai people immediately exerts its old fascination on me. There's everything under the sun on sale: calabash gourds in every shape and size, masks, carved figurines, paintings and brightly coloured Masai jewellery of every sort. I have no trouble whatsoever getting rid of my money.

That evening I'm suddenly seized by the desire to cook for my hosts. Nice as it is not to have to cook every day, it dawns on me that back home in Switzerland I enjoy making dinner for my daughter and me. And so Klaus, Irene and I spend a pleasant evening in, chatting about the next day's trip to Mombasa before we go to bed, last stop on my sentimental journey.

Mombasa

As we get off the plane in Mombasa we're met by the same warm humid tropical air that I first fell in love with, the same scent of the sea. It's only been a short internal flight but even so the impression is of being in a completely different country. Klaus has done the groundwork in advance and so we have a well-respected local taxi driver waiting for us. He'll be at our disposal for the next day and a half, which is all the time I have left to revisit my memories.

First of all we head for the old part of town where all the fruit and vegetable markets are. Kenya's second biggest city has a Muslim feel to it: alongside African women dressed in European clothes are veiled women in black. The pace of life here is less hectic than in Nairobi, however, and at last I feel happy getting about on foot. I wander through the old part of town breathing in the exotic air, with its rich mix of sea salt, fruit, vegetables and spices. The huge sacks of red, orange, yellow and black ground spices are a feast for both eyes and nose. Fruit here has a rich intense smell that we never experience in a supermarket back in Europe. People keep asking me to taste some. Women sit under an umbrella to shade them from the scorching sun and offer their vegetables for sale. What would Mama say if she could see all this?

I stroll down to Fort Jesus, a fortress built by the Portuguese in 1593, enjoying the light breeze that blows through my clothing. In the distance I can make out the Likoni ferry where my African fate first took its course. Tomorrow I will board it once again. For today it's too late and we make our way to a hotel on the outskirts of the city.

The Likoni Ferry

Our driver picks us up after breakfast. Unfortunately it's been raining a little and the sky is overcast. We drive along the northern coast towards the city and then head directly for the ferry. A long queue of cars and lorries and hundreds of people are already waiting for the ferry to dock. It's always a frantic business, even though the crossing itself only takes a few minutes. Watching the ferry go through its docking manoeuvres, I realize that this one is slightly larger than the one on which my fate was decided. And then the horde piles on board, carrying me with them.

Klaus and I are the only white people among the more than five hundred on the ferry – just like it was eighteen years ago when my boyfriend Marco and I were the only tourists on board. I climb up to the upper deck and let my gaze sweep out over the heads of the heaving masses towards the open sea, lost in contemplation of all the events my first journey on this ferry unleashed. Who would have thought back then that this one fateful event would not only set my life on a completely different course but also come to move many others all over the world? Standing there by the railing, I'm lost in amazement at the turns my life has taken. I turn around and – irony of ironies – find myself staring into the eyes of a young Masai warrior barely fifteen feet away. He is neither as tall nor as handsome as Lketinga was back then, but even so this one moment brings all my old feelings and all my memories rushing back. My heart starts beating faster once more and I close my eyes and see myself as I was back then, a pretty 26-year-old woman turning her head at my then boyfriend's suggestion and looking into the proud eyes of the man who would become my husband. I can see Lketinga standing there: tall, gracious, exotic and unbelievably beautiful, his face painted, his long red hair plaited finely and his naked torso adorned with necklaces of beads. Just the sight of him took my breath away and swept me off my feet.

Klaus brings me back from my dreams to ask if I've noticed the Masai standing behind me. 'Of course,' I tell him with a laugh, 'but I'm pleased to say you're not Marco and our young warrior here isn't Lketinga.'

Before long the ferry docks and we walk across to the taxi that will take us to the Diani coast. Along the route I try to make out where our old souvenir shop would have been, but it's not easy – so much has changed. Everywhere I look there's new building going on. Where there was once empty bush country, there are now golf courses, hotels and apartment complexes.

It's only on the third time along the same stretch of road that I finally spot our white building, but to my disappointment there are no longer any shops there. It seems the whole block has been turned into apartments, and the entire complex in turn has been surrounded by a security fence. I don't know what I'd expected but I'm still disappointed that everything has altered so far beyond recognition.

We drive on to the Africa Sea Lodge, the hotel where I stayed the first time – still a tourist – I came to Mombasa. I suppose I was hoping I might find Priscilla on the beach. She was the one I lived with for a few months that first time in Mombasa, and she was a great help to me. A few tourists had told me she was still there, selling kangas. But with the rain beginning to fall again, my hopes were fading. When we get to the hotel I see that the side of the street opposite has completely changed. There are now several roads heading off into the bush and I can see a school in the distance. Almost certainly Kamau village where I spent my last six months in Kenya is not there anymore. That's something we can't check out so easily, however, as the rain has already turned the roads to mud. We walk into the hotel grounds. These at least have changed little, although there are a lot fewer tourists than there used to be.

We have coffee and then suddenly the sun breaks through again. I kick off my sandals and run along the beach in my bare feet. A few of the beach hawkers approach me; a few others simply stand there selling their masks and paintings. That is where I sat after my first 'unsuccessful' kiss with Lketinga, and again three years later when our young daughter was playing on the sand. This is also where we sat with Papa Saguna the first time he saw the sea and was almost sick with terror. I give free rein to all my memories, feelings and thoughts and let my feet bury themselves in the sand. Once again it comes home to me how strong my fascination with this country is, and in particular that part of it that is hardest to love – the Samburu lands. But at the same time I feel I have neither the ability nor the desire to live in Kenya anymore either in Samburu country or here on the coast.

There is nothing left for me in Mombasa now and I feel glad when we're on our way to the airport. Once again I find myself on the Likoni ferry, and once again I realize my knees will always go weak here, whether or not there's a Masai anywhere to be seen. Here feelings overwhelm me that I simply cannot explain, even today. Even so, I can honestly and sincerely say that of all the adventures, emotions and risks I went through here, I regret not one.

I am happy that I have such a wonderful African family and I regard it as a great gift to have been allowed to come back after fourteen years and be welcomed once again into their midst.

But now it's time to go home, to my daughter. Right now, all I want to do is to throw my arms around her and tell her about her family in Africa, the family she still doesn't know.

Charity donations for Kenya

For several years now my German publishers A1 Verlag and I have supported my Kenyan family in Barsaloi. This has also helped other Samburu living in the area. Nonetheless, there remains a lot of extreme poverty in this part of northern Kenya.

Should readers wish to donate, after much careful research and evaluation I have decided to recommend the following organization

Eine-Welt-Verein Keniahilfe e.V.
Schwardwaldstrasse 80
77815 B¸hl-Neusatz
keniahilfe@web.de

This organization works for the common good and has for many years been involved with concrete projects in Northern Kenya, including education, health and self-help schemes, always in close cooperation with responsible local officials.

Every donation goes in its entirety to the aid projects. In contrast with many other aid organizations, no administration costs are deducted.

In Barsaloi

These donations provide material support for many of the Samburu families amongst whom I lived. The local school for boys and girls receives direct aid, as do poor people who have no other access to medical care.

Sererit

Everyone who read my first book needs no introduction to Father Giuliani. I hold him in the highest esteem, not just because I personally owe him a huge debt but also because of his intelligent and worthwhile work among the Samburu in the remote Ndoto Mountains. He set up the little Mission at Sererit with the most basic of means at his disposal and remains ready to help anyone and everyone wherever he can make a difference.

If you wish to make a donation to one of these projects in particular, please mention the word 'Barsaloi' or 'Sererit'. If, however, you wish to contribute to both, simply use both words (Barsaloi/Sererit).
Bank details:

Eine-Welt-Verein Keniafilfe e.V.
Sparkasse B¸hl
Account number 49 007
Sort code: 662 514 34

For donations from Switzerland or Austria or other countries outside Germany, the international references are:

IBAN: DE826625143000049007
BIC: SOLA DE S1 BHL

The organization Eine-Welt-Verein e.V. is a recognized charity and obviously you will receive a written acknowledgement of your donation.